Presidential

PICTURE STORIES

Behind the Cameras
at the White House

Presidential

PICTURE STORIES

Behind the Cameras
at the White House

Dennis Brack

ISBN # 978-0-615-64882-8

Current printing (last digit) 10 9 8 7 6 5 4 3 2 1

Book design and production by David and Hannah Kleber.

Credit for cover photographs (clockwise): President Ford, David Hume Kennerly; President Kennedy, Abbie Rowe, Department of Interior, LOC; President Truman, Abbie Rowe, Department of Interior, LOC.

ACKNOWLEDGEMENTS

Arthur Scott worked as a photographer for Hearst's International News Photos and then went to the Hill as a photographer for the United States Senate. He realized the importance of writing down the stories of the photographers in the first part of the twentieth century. Without Arthur Scott, the history of the first years of the White House News Photographers Association would have been lost.

Arthur Scott

David Kleber was hired by NBC for his technical knowledge of the complicated electrical equipment. He started as what the old timers called a "soundman" (translation: audio technician). He was the man behind the man with the camera who made the equipment work. He eventually became a cameraman for NBC and one of "the men behind the cameras at the White House." David retired but remains an active member of the WHNPA. David and his wife, Hannah Kleber, an award-winning artist with more than thirty-five years' experience in design and production, used their knowledge and talent to unite the stories and pictures of this book into the attractive work that you hold in your hands.

Months before this book went to the printer, I thought that I was finished. Friends read the book and thought that I was not. Doug Daniel edited my words, pulled these stories together and, as my son, Dennis, would say, "saved me from myself." Thank you, Doug.

Finally, the photographers. Hundreds of great photographers have walked through the doors of the White House and many are the subjects of stories in this book. A larger book could tell the stories of Harry Van Tine, Murray Alvey, George Dorsey, Bill Smith, Charlie Mack, L.C. Brown, Harvey Georges, Dennis Cook, Ray Lustig, Kevin Gilbert, Ron Bennett, and Bernie Boston. There are great photographers working today with loads of stories: Chip Somodevilla, Charles Dharapak, Susan Walsh, Jim Watson, Scottie Applewhite, Ron Sachs, Jonathan Ernst, Kevin Lamarque, Jim Lo Scalzo, Pablo Martinez Monsivais, John McDonnell, and Brendan Smialowski. They will be the source of stories for another book written by someone like me in the years to come.

CONTENTS

INTRODUCTION

FOOT SOLDIERS OF HISTORY

Credit: U.S. National Archives

On the morning of February 27, 1860, a relatively unknown ex-congressman named Abraham Lincoln walked into photographer Mathew Brady's studio at 634 Broadway in New York. In preparing the homely, clean-shaven politician for a portrait, Brady drew up Lincoln's collar in an effort to improve his appearance. Then Brady made his picture. The result, historian Mary Panzer noted, was a portrait of a firm, determined Lincoln who had the look of a statesman.

That evening at New York's Cooper Union, Lincoln delivered

Mathew Brady. Photo: U.S. National Archives.

an address about his views opposing slavery. His argument for prohibiting the spread of slavery into the western territories ignited his Republican audience. Lincoln later went to the offices of the *New York Tribune* to proofread his speech, determined that every word appear correctly. Lincoln did not deliver many speeches during the presidential election. His standard response to questions about issues was, "Read my Cooper Union speech."

The speech also made Brady's portrait of Lincoln one of his best-selling *cartes de visite*. These albumen prints, at two and a half inches by four inches, were widely circulated in the 1860's. The magazine *Harper's Weekly* used a woodcut of the portrait for a cover story on Lincoln. Other publications used Brady's photograph to illustrate stories about the Illinois lawyer who was discussed as a possible Republican nominee for president.

Just over a year later, Lincoln was president and leading the nation in a civil war against the South. Brady wanted to document the upcoming hostilities, but he was afraid that his traveling darkroom would not be permitted to pass through Union lines. He took advantage of Lincoln's appreciation of his work. Shortly before the Battle of Bull Run, the first major battle of the war, Brady walked over to the White House and told Lincoln of his fear of being detained. The president listened and then wrote on a thick card, "Pass Brady. A Lincoln." It may have been the first "total access" press pass, the result of a unique collaboration between a president and a photographer.

The longtime chronicler of presidents for *Time* and *Life* magazines, writer Hugh Sidey, observed, "Photographers are the foot soldiers of history." Reporters and historians can produce their work with second-hand accounts, but photographers have to be

Hal Hall, Harry M. Van Tine, J.C. Brown, Alley West, Arthur Leonard, Tommy Baltzell, Frank Cullen, George Dorsey, Reeves W.M. Gardner, Chas. Simon, White House policeman. Photo: National Photo Company, Library of Congress.

there to make their pictures.

With their assignments to make pictures comes waiting—and waiting is one of the things that photographers do very well. The wait could be at a courthouse door as the felon *du jour* prepares to emerge and walk to a limousine. It could be at a newsroom preparing for a story to break. Or it could be the wait for a tardy president.

In these long hours of boredom, photographers tell stories. Most stories are about the people in our business, and if you are around long enough you hear the same story told many times but with different heroes or villains, but they are still good stories. Sometimes we have all heard the story many times, but we let the storyteller go on right to the end. Often the storyteller has more fun than the audience.

The photographers covering the White House have always had the close-in views of presidential administrations that no one else in the media can get. And they have their own stories to tell. Generally

New Orleans, the Presidential Campaign in June 1976. A morning coffee with some of the best photographers (and best friends) of the seventies. Left to right: Charles Tasnadi, Associated Press; Wally McNamee, Newsweek; *Dirck Halstead,* TIME; *David Hume Kennerly, White House Photographer; Dennis Brack, Black Star; Bob Sherman, freelance; David Burnett, Contact; Paul Slade,* Paris Match; *Terry DeWitt, ABC.*

their stories have never been recorded, but they are told and retold in the White House press work area over the years.

This book is a collection of such stories, most of them told by or about members of the White House News Photographers Association. Many of the stories are about events that I witnessed or participated in. As a photojournalist for more than fifty years I have worked with the top photographers of our time. In the sixties I listened to photographers talk about the great photographers whom they met when they were young, and in the following decades I have watched great photojournalists work and listened to their stories.

Today's hot photojournalists do what the early greats did: Make pictures and get them out as fast as possible. Their stories are part of the photographer's lore, part of what makes taking pictures for a living so much fun.

Those 'Picturemen' at the White House

Woodrow Wilson, Warren G. Harding, Calvin Coolidge, Herbert Hoover

Severe headaches forced President Woodrow Wilson to return to the White House in the middle of a nationwide tour to promote the ratification of the League of Nations Treaty. On October 2, 1919, the president suffered a massive, debilitating stroke—not that the public knew about it.

"Wilson Watch" cameramen take a time out to pose for a group photograph on West Executive Avenue. Photo: National Photo Company, Library of Congress.

The rush of doctors and medical equipment to the White House alerted the press that Wilson had a major health problem. Few knew the status of the president's illness. The first lady, Edith Wilson, and Dr. Cary T. Grayson, Wilson's physician, friend, and adviser, were not talking.

For months it was a mystery: Just who was running the country? The news photographers in Washington were feeling great pressure from their editors to get a photograph of Wilson.

In the spring of 1920, rumors of Wilson taking a bit of sun on the South Lawn of the White House sent photographers roaming around the fence of the South Lawn and at the gate of West Executive Avenue. No luck.

A flock of sheep grazed on the South Lawn, and every morning workmen rolled a wagonload of hay through the gate for the sheep to munch. Early one morning a photographer, H. M. Van Tine, and a colleague climbed under the hay in an effort to get close enough for the highly sought photograph of Wilson in his wheelchair. A Secret

Sheep graze on the South Lawn in 1919. Photo: Harris & Ewing, Library of Congress.

A load of hay on East Executive Avenue. Photo: National Photo Company, Library of Congress.

Service agent noticed that the hay was a bit lumpy and began poking a stick into the load. It was back to the West Executive Avenue curb for Van Tine and his friend.

Even in his healthier days, Wilson was not interested in being photographed outside of his official duties. After his marriage to Edith Galt in December 1915, his honeymoon in Hot Springs, Virginia, was a major story. Every photographer wanted a piece of it, but President Wilson did not want to see honeymoon pictures in the newspapers or the movie houses. The president told Dick Jervis, the head of his Secret Service detail, that if anyone got a picture, he would be fired.

President Wilson played golf every day, and Jervis had an idea. He called the photographers together to suggest that they should go to a shack near one of the golf greens. It was full of knotholes, he told them, through which pictures could be made. That afternoon, the cameramen crowded into the shack and began looking for the best positions and the largest knotholes. But there were none—and no way out, for as soon as all the boys were inside, Jervis padlocked the door.

The president played his golf game undisturbed. Facing a crowd of angry cameramen after Wilson had finished, Jervis explained, "You know that I try to give you every break on pictures, but the boss said no, so what could I do?"

As Wilson recovered slightly that summer of 1920, White House officials called on photographer George Harris to make a photograph of the president at work to prove to the nation that he

President Wilson and first lady Edith Wilson pose for a photograph to prove that the president is in good health. Photo: Harris & Ewing, Library of Congress.

President Wilson takes a ride in the presidential limousine for the cameramen. Photo: Joe Roberts, WHNPA.

could perform his presidential duties. The situation was highly controlled by Mrs. Wilson. Close examination of the photograph shows that the first lady had to assist the president because his paralyzed arm could not steady the document.

The pressure for additional views of Wilson continued. The photographers gathered outside the White House gates to make pictures of the president and first lady during their afternoon automobile rides. The head of the Secret Service observed their efforts and remarked, "You picturemen ought to band together."

Photographers circa 1920. Photo: National Photo Company, Library of Congress.

For the first half of the twentieth century, photographers came up through the ranks at newspapers. They were generally copyboys with little or no education. If a city editor was impressed with a copyboy who was smart and aggressive, he would send him over to photo. He would start as a "squeegee boy" who dried the prints or a "gofer" who helped the newspaper photographers on their assignments and ran the film back to the paper. He would learn the trade from the older photographers. Historians William Hannigan and Ken Johnston noted that photographers in that period were usually

Teddy Johnson working in darkroom. Photo: National Photo Company, Library of Congress.

considered technicians who operated the cameras and enlargers that produced the photographs that "described" the scene, not people actually making journalism.

President Harding and the first lady at the North Portico. Photo: National Photo Company, Library of Congress.

The copyboys who became photographers were rough men. When they were on the street their creed was to "make it work" to get the picture. A photographer working back then, Woodrow "Woody" Wilson, learned quickly that "the boss is paying you for pictures, not excuses." The order of the day for Arthur

Ellis, a photographer for the *Washington Post*, was simple: "Get it first and get it best."

Twenty-four movie and still photographers working in Washington took the advice of the president's Secret Service chief. On June 13, 1921, they met in the office of the National Photo Company and formed the White House News Photographers Association. They represented Harris & Ewing, International Newsreel, National Photo Company, Atlantic & Pacific, Underwood & Underwood, Keystone View Company, Associated Screen News, Fox News Corporation, Pathe News Corporation, the *Washington Post*, the *Washington Times*, and the *Washington Star*. The beginning of the Warren G. Harding administration was the perfect time to organize. Harding's secretary, George B. Christian, recognized the association immediately.

The "picturemen" were together, but they were still standing at the gates of the White House on West Executive Avenue, in that day an active street for automobile and pedestrian traffic. Harding began to notice this group of grown men as he walked back to the White House after lunch each day. At first he thought that they were just tourists. Finally, he asked someone and learned that they were the photographers and that they were permitted on the White House grounds only on special occasions.

Harding was a newspaperman, the publisher of the *Marion Daily Star* in Marion, Ohio, and the only newspaper publisher to become

President Harding showing "first dog" Laddie Boy to newspaper correspondents in 1921.

president. He decided that the photographers were journalists just like the reporters and should have the same access to the White House. A small wooden shed was built near the West Wing door for the photographers and their equipment.

Harding knew the value of a good human-interest story. When an Airedale named Laddie Boy arrived as a gift for the new president, Harding stopped his Cabinet meeting and went out to meet the dog who would become the White House mascot. Within minutes the president and his new friend were walking around the White House grounds and posing for photographs. A series of "First Dog" stories helped make Laddie Boy the first famous presidential pet. In the years

President Harding with photographers during U.S. Marine Corps maneuvers on the Gettysburg battlefield in 1922. Photo: H. (Pappy) Van Tine, National Photo Company; Library of Congress.

that followed, his exploits were a bit of good news amid the scandals that embroiled the Harding administration.

Harding himself was a good subject. He was cooperative and thought of as a regular fellow by the photographers. "We went with Harding down in Virginia when they reenacted the Battle of the

Vice President Coolidge posing with Indian tribal leaders on the South Lawn. Photo: Harris & Ewing, Library of Congress.

President Coolidge and the reels. Photo: Library of Congress.

The newsreel cameraman was a big deal in the thirties. Photo: Harris & Ewing, Library of Congress.

Wilderness," photographer Buck May said. "I remember some of us were sitting around one night in our tent playing poker. Suddenly the tent flap opened and President Harding stuck his head in and asked if anybody had a chew of tobacco. We asked him to stay and play with us. He said he would have liked to but had to get back to his tent."

Photographers would always have better luck in covering a president who had been a senator or a vice president. The photographers had shared experiences and become friends with the subject. The former senator or vice president had already learned the drill: Take a few seconds to work with the guys, give them the pictures they need, and the day goes smoothly.

That was the case with Calvin Coolidge. A big part of the job when Coolidge was Harding's vice president was to do some menial tasks that the president was too busy to attend to. The photographers found that Coolidge always had time to have his picture taken. After he had become president, someone asked Coolidge what he did for exercise. He pointed to the photographers and said, "I do what the photographers ask me to do and that's plenty of exercise."

Perhaps Coolidge understood the power of the picture news—especially the newsreels. Seen across the United States in movie theaters, they were the only way that the public could view moving pictures of news events. The newsreel photographers used 35mm motion picture film, which was expensive and difficult to work with, and they were respected journalists in the White House press room. In the new era of moving images, they were called "the reels" while the still photographers were "the stills."

Coolidge was a movie fan, watching a film nearly every night, and the newsreels were his favorite part of each evening. He thought that they were important for keeping the public informed of current events.

On June 4, 1927, while reviewing Navy ships at Hampton Roads, Virginia, Coolidge was not too pleased with the work of one still photographer. On the deck of the presidential yacht, the USS *Mayflower*, Coolidge had spent hours standing at the ship's rail and saluting the ships as they passed by. He grew tired and sat down, but the ships kept passing in review. The president just sat and saluted.

The sitting president salutes. Photo: Buck May, Harris & Ewing; Library of Congress.

Photographer Buck May took a picture of Coolidge sitting and saluting. Immediately the president turned to May and sternly asked, "Why'd you take a picture like that

Mrs. Coolidge works her movie camera.
Photo: National Photo Company, Library of
Congress.

for?" In spite of the president's admonition, May put out the photograph. It was printed the next day in the *Washington Star* and many other newspapers across the nation, becoming one of the signature photographs of the Coolidge years. The president declined to seek re-election, and May continued working for five more decades.

First lady Grace Coolidge liked photography and the photographers. And the photographers liked her, making her an honorary member of the White House News Photographers Association. One of Johnny Di Joseph's very first assignments in his seventy-year career

President Hoover at his automobile on West Executive Avenue. Photo: Harris &
Ewing, Library of Congress.

was to cover the president returning from church services. Coolidge and the first lady came out of the church and walked down the steps, but Di Joseph missed the picture. His face must have shown it. Mrs. Coolidge stopped and asked if everything was all right. He confessed that he had missed the picture. "Don't worry," Mrs. Coolidge assured him. "We'll just do it again." She grabbed her husband and walked back up the church steps and then came down again. Di Joseph got his picture.

The first lady did not accompany her husband to the White House News Photographers Association dinner. They were always stag occasions in those days, and Coolidge brought along an aide instead of his wife. The photographers could not afford to pay for entertainment so they persuaded talent from the local vaudeville houses to come over and perform between acts. The headliner for the evening was named Gilda Gray. "She came in that grass skirt," photographer Hugh Miller recalled years later. "She was the shimmy girl and did a hell of a dance for us."

Spirited applause led to a half-dozen curtain calls. "Wait a minute, fellows, wait a minute," Gilda Gray told her appreciative audience. "You haven't seen nothing yet." With that, Coolidge turned to his aide and said, "Get my hat."

The photographers needed all the help that they could find during the Hoover administration. President Herbert Hoover was a tough subject, harboring a nervous dislike of the cameras. "He had a rather square face with small features," photographer George Harris remembered, "and he was not sufficiently interested in showing to good advantage to be helpful to the man behind the lens." To some photographers, Hoover seemed as if he was afraid he was going to say something he was not supposed to say.

Some presidents excited crowds—not Hoover. He was not known for his charisma. J.C. Brown, an MGM movie cameraman, remembered that when Hoover was traveling, the crowds just stood and stared. Brown used to yell at people, "Wave, smile, cheer—do something besides stare."

President Hoover wears one of his "horse collar shirts." Photo: Harris & Ewing, Library of Congress.

First lady Lou Henry Hoover. Photo: Harris & Ewing, Library of Congress.

To photographer Johnny Di Joseph, the problem at the White House was not the president. "He was okay," Di Joseph recalled. "It was his wife." First lady Lou Henry Hoover was made an honorary member of the White House News Photographers Association, too, but that did not make her the photographers' friend. Di Joseph remembered that Mrs. Hoover had a rule that no photographer could come within fifteen feet of her husband to make a picture. The president wore two-inch high collars with his shirts—Di Joseph called them "horse collars." Mrs. Hoover did not like the way the president's double chins fell over his collar, and she thought that keeping the photographers at a distance would prevent them from making close-up photographs emphasizing his weight.

Newsmagazines carried stories about trouble between the cameramen, the White House correspondents, and Hoover. The president and the photographers waged a major battle over covering the president doing what he liked to do the most—fishing. The first volleys had been fired shortly after Hoover was nominated for president. Campaign aides wanted to show their candidate as a regular fellow and invited photographers to a spot on the Rogue River in Oregon where Hoover and a friend were fishing. Photographers lined the banks and splashed around to get a better angle on Hoover as he waded in the

Mrs. Hoover poses a group of Girl Scouts on the South Lawn. Photo: National Photo Company, Library of Congress.

middle of the stream. Some photographers commandeered a boat and rowed out to where Hoover was casting. That was it. Hoover was through fishing for that day. When a photographer on the shore asked for a close-up, the candidate curtly replied, "You shall not have one."

Hoover fished throughout his presidency and actually created a presidential retreat around his fishing passion. Camp Rapidan, or Camp Hoover, was about three and a half hours south of Washington in what would become Shenandoah National Park. Staff members later recounted how the president actually helped in moving the rocks in the river to create pools for the trout. The press was banned from Camp Hoover. The president maintained that "fish will not bite in the presence of the representatives of the press."

It is an irony that the president who disliked photographers and their photographs would be the subject of the first candid photographs of a president. Erich Salomon, a German photographer who liked to be described as a photojournalist, came to Washington in 1931 and created quite a stir among the news photographers. There were rules about where you could and could not take pictures—and Salomon broke every one of them. Using a small camera with a fast lens (Ermanox, Zeiss Ikon 100mm f/2) and available light, Salomon would walk into the visitors' galleries of the Senate and the Supreme

President Hoover at his favorite pastime: fishing. Photo: National Photo Company, Library of Congress.

Court and make pictures even though cameras were not allowed.

The Washington regulars did not embrace Salomon's style. The WHNPA minutes from a 1932 meeting noted, "Mr. De Tilta appointed himself a committee of one to investigate the activities of Dr. Salomon, the German photographer who is residing at the Mayflower Hotel and making a nuisance of himself at public functions."

Salomon persuaded his friend French Premier Pierre Laval to permit him to come along for a meeting with Hoover. The session was anything but the candid scene that Salomon had envisioned. The photographer kept trying for more and the White House usher at Salomon's elbow kept nudging and encouraging him to "make it snappy."

Erich Salomon

Photographer George Tames remembered little of value coming out of the White House during the Hoover years. "Up to that time, photography was very limited," Tames said. "There are very few pictures of Hoover in action, or in the White House."

All that was about to change.

THE GREATEST
PICTURE SUBJECT OF ALL

FRANKLIN D. ROOSEVELT

The news photographers covering President Franklin D. Roosevelt played by rules that today's photojournalists find difficult to understand. Yet those rules came with access to the White House that news photographers had never enjoyed before.

When Roosevelt replaced Herbert Hoover in March 1933, only fifteen or so news photographers—both "the stills" and "the reels"—covered the White House. Roosevelt's press secretary, Steve Early, brought them together for a meeting. A young photographer at the time, George Tames recalled Early telling them: "President Roosevelt is crippled. There's nothing secret

Statue of President Roosevelt in a wheelchair at the FDR Memorial in Washington. Photo: Dennis Brack.

about that. And he has a favor to ask of his friends in the media, his photographic friends, and that is not to photograph him when he's being carried, or when he is in some of the more compromising positions. In return, the president pledges to make himself more available to the photographers."

Roosevelt had issued his first rules to photographers during his campaign for governor of New York. They were not to take any photographs of the candidate looking crippled or helpless from the polio that had paralyzed his legs a few years earlier. A newsreel film of Roosevelt in 1928, the year he ran for governor, shows him in a car and telling the photographers, "No movies of me getting out the machine, boys."

The rules for photographers at the White House were clear: No pictures of the president in leg braces, on crutches, or in a wheelchair, and no pictures of the president getting into or out of a vehicle, which highlighted his paralysis and need for assistance. "You follow the rules," Early assured them, "you'll get your pictures."

A small elevator was installed to lift President Roosevelt onto his airplane, The Sacred Cow. The Airplane is on display at Wright Patterson Air Force Base, Dayton, Ohio. Photo: Dennis Brack.

Not only was Early's pitch on behalf of Roosevelt not new, it followed four years of limited access to Hoover. "So the photographers agreed to his request," Tames said, "but something happened. Within two or three years, what had been a request had the effect of law."

The photographers at the White House honored the rules— they even kept each other in line. "If, as it happened once or twice, one of its members sought to violate it and try to sneak a picture of the president in his chair," historian Hugh Gregory Gallagher wrote, "one or another of the older photographers would 'accidentally' knock the camera to the ground or otherwise block the picture."

None of the photographers who covered the Roosevelt White House interviewed for this book recalled a photographer even attempting to make a photograph of Roosevelt in his wheelchair. It just was not done. "I asked once to see a copy of the rules," George Tames wrote in a memoir, "and was informed by one of the older hands that if I wanted to be a wiseass who didn't follow the rules, then they would see that I never made a picture around the White House again."

One exception of a press photographer trying to make a picture of Roosevelt in his wheelchair was *Life* magazine's George Skadding. He had been the Associated Press photographer covering the White House for years before joining the *Life* staff. His editors wanted to run a photograph of Roosevelt being carried by an aide and gave the awkward assignment to Skadding. He tried many ways, using short and long lenses, and did get a picture. Early's office threatened to pull his press credentials.

Early kept a tight rein on the photographers. Knowing that flashbulbs blinded Roosevelt and made him quite uncomfortable, Early issued an order that pictures were only to be made when he gave the word, "Shoot."

Congress had its own rules, forbidding photography in the House and Senate chambers. Photographer Jackie Martin earned a reputation for making pictures anyway. One of the few female news photographers in Washington during Roosevelt's administration, Martin was the art director and picture editor of the *Washington Times Herald*, the first woman to oversee those departments at a big-city newspaper. An historian of the period wrote that Martin had "the daring and fearlessness of the male news photographer."

Martin was also among the first news photographers in the capitol to see the merits of 35mm cameras for news coverage, using the small camera to take pictures at events that had never been photographed. She managed to sneak in a camera to photograph the funeral service, in 1936, of Speaker Jo Byrns in the House of Representatives. When she secretly photographed Cabinet members listening to Roosevelt speaking at the opening of Congress, the pictures ran as a full-page spread on the front page of the *Times Herald*. Martin had made her pictures from a seat in the press box. The telephones rang with protests from the news organizations she had bested.

More rules for photographing Roosevelt came with World War II. A press blackout was in place for the president's movements, which

Steve Early, holding papers, keeps a sharp eye on the photographers during a photo session with the president. Photo: Abbie Rowe, National Archives.

were not reported even if known. Roosevelt could be away from the White House for long periods of time. Associated Press photographer Henry Burroughs recalled how, in 1945, Secret Service agents said that the president had been driven to Shangri-La, the presidential retreat in Maryland now named Camp David. It was announced later that, in fact, Roosevelt had traveled to the Soviet city of Yalta for a conference with British Prime Minister Winston Churchill and Soviet leader Joseph Stalin.

In spite of all the rules, the Roosevelt years were happy times for the news photographers covering the White House. The president photographed like a million dollars and seemed to enjoy facing the barrage of cameras. He was a handsome man so it was easy to make a good picture of him. One photographer observed at the time, "It's pictures we're after and Franklin Delano Roosevelt was the greatest picture subject."

Photographer George Tames thought Roosevelt's success with photographers was because, like any great politician, he was a show-man. He used what vaudeville folks called "shtick"—a device that would capture the attention of his audience and take their eyes off of what was actually happening.

Entering a banquet room, for example, was very difficult for Roosevelt. When he came into the room he would have his hand on an aide's arm for support as he swung his paralyzed, braced legs in a kind of walking movement. He would stop at tables and lean over to talk to someone who was seated. Those stops were ar-ranged in advance and the people were told to stay in their chairs. The president would grasp the person's shoulder or perhaps the arm of the chair and earnestly talk to the seated person—a mo-ment or two to rest before moving on. The distraction of the stops to chat made people unaware of his braces and would leave them thinking that they had seen the president gracefully enter the room. It was a great act.

For the photographers, the "shtick" was Roosevelt's cigarette holder, a pen, perhaps the tilt of his head. If a particular pose did not work, the president would suggest, "Let's try one this way," and they would make their shot. A good picture was what the photographers were after. And Roosevelt seemed happy to see them. Photographer Arthur Scott remembered, "It was seldom that they entered his of-fice that they were not greeted with some cheerful remark." As the photographers filed into the Oval Office and prepared to make their pictures, the president would chat a bit. He followed the horses and might ask which horse they liked for a race at Pimlico, the Baltimore race track.

Arthur Scott shows President Roosevelt the four finalists in the WHNPA contest. The president picked the photograph nearest to him as the first-place winner.

The wire service photographers assigned to the White House guarded their beat jealously. There was no rotation and the president saw the same photographers day after day. Roosevelt did not call them by their given names, but he did make up nicknames for some of "the boys"—in those days, when they were in a group, photographers were often referred to as boys. Roosevelt called Pacific and Atlantic photographer Woodrow Wilson "Mr. President" because of his name. To everyone else he was "Woody."

A photographer Roosevelt did know by his first name was Johnny Thompson of Acme News Service. Thompson was a tricky fellow. He and all the other photographers used 4x5 Speed Graphic cameras, loading the film in the back with a film holder containing two sheets of film. After one exposure, the photographer would slide out the holder, turn it, and slide it back in for the second exposure. Additional film holders might be kept in a coat pocket. Thompson took advantage of the process by waiting until the other photogra-

President Roosevelt signs the declaration of war against Germany as Senator Tom Connally notes the time. Photo: Farm Security Administration and Office of War Information Collection, Library of Congress.

phers had made a picture and, when they were busy changing their film holders, asking the president to do something that would make a much better picture.

Congress declared war on Japan for the attack on Pearl Harbor on December 7, 1941, and declared war on Germany a few days later. The photographers were called into the Oval Office to photograph Roosevelt signing the declaration of war against Germany. Sure enough, all the photographers made their pictures and were changing holders on their 4x5 Graphics. Thompson did not shoot that first holder and quickly asked Senator Tom Connally, who was standing over the president's shoulder, to hold his pocket watch to get the exact time, and to lean in closer to the president during the signing. Thompson took his picture and immediately said, "Thank you, Mr. President," the signal that indicated that the picture session was over. His picture was the one used in the papers the next morning.

On December 7, 1941, Associated Press photographer Max Desfor had been covering the Redskins-Eagles football game in Griffith Stadium in Washington. He was in a special press box on the fifty-yard line. The box was positioned below the loge seats and held four or five photographers. Desfor was sitting behind a camera called a "Big Bertha," a Speed Graphic with a long telephoto that used 5x7 sheets of film. During the first half of the game he heard a series of messages over the stadium public address system telling colonels and admirals to call their offices. He knew something was up and at halftime called the AP bureau from a pay phone. "Max," he was told, "get your ass back here. We've been attacked!"

As soon as Max returned to the AP bureau he was told to go to the State Department. At that time the State Department was in the Old Executive Office Building, now called the Eisenhower Executive Office Building. He rushed to the bottom of the steps just as Japanese diplomats Kichisaburo Nomura and Saburo Kurusu were leaving the building. Secretary of State Cordell Hull was following them, extremely angry and berating the diplomats in a loud voice. Desfor made pictures, rushed back to the AP bureau, and was told to get to the Japanese Embassy.

When Desfor arrived at the Japanese Embassy, on Massachusetts Avenue, he found photographer Tom O'Halloran of Harris and Ewing and other photographers in the courtyard. They were making pictures of the embassy staff burning top-secret documents. The staff tried to prevent the photographers from making pictures by coming at them with brooms. Without any planning, the photographers broke up into two groups. While the Japanese staff chased one group with their brooms, the other group would make pictures. Desfor would see one of the Japanese diplomats again—nearly four years later, on the deck of the USS *Missouri* as Japanese officials signed the document of surrender that ended World War II.

Soon, Desfor walked out of the AP bureau in the *Washington Star* building and turned the corner to be fitted for a smart brown military uniform. The wire service and *Life*

Sergeant Wes Howland

magazine photographers were part of a still photographic pool. Their pictures would go to all publications at no charge and the government would pay for their transportation, food, and housing. These photographers had the privileges of a

Bert Brandt, Ollie Atkins, and William Allen in Paris.

captain, which meant that they could eat in the officers' mess and stay in officers' housing, but they could not order anyone around. They did have an insignia on the arm of the uniform that resembled the patch of a major, but it had a "C" in the middle for correspondent. Soldiers would approach Desfor, start to salute, take a closer look and spot the "C." There would be a small murmur—*"shit"*—and a rapid end to the salute.

Other photographers were going to war, too. *Washington Post* photographers Joe Heiberger and Wes Howland put on Marine Corps uniforms. Johnny Thompson of Acme—Roosevelt always called him "that man"—went to flight school. Ollie Atkins headed to Northern Africa for the Red Cross.

Roberta Barrett photographs President Roosevelt. Photo: WHNPA.

As in many professions, the men heading to the battlefields left vacancies in jobs at home. It was the same in the news business. Jackie Martin landed a job with the *Chicago Sun*. In February 1942, she became the first of many women to become members of the White House News Photographers Association. Maria Hanson, *Life* magazine, and Marion Carpenter and Roberta Barrett, International News Photos, soon joined the WHNPA.

Photographers abroad covered men fighting and dying. Edward Widdis, an AP photographer on the New Guinea front, sent back a note to his fellow photographers: "I've seen things that I hope I never have to talk about, and I can understand now why World War I veterans were always reluctant about telling of their experiences. The beautiful and amusing things we'll try to remember, and the horrors we will try to forget."

Herbert White of the AP and William Forsythe, making pictures for the Coast Guard, were in the first landings in Sicily. The prize for landing ingenuity went to Bert Brandt of Acme for being in the first wave to hit the Normandy beaches. Brandt jumped into the water and while under fierce machine gun fire managed to photograph everything. He made pictures of three more waves of troops coming ashore and then waded back and climbed on an empty landing craft. From there he went to a troop ship back to an English port. Brandt persuaded an officer to give him a jeep and driver for the three-hour trip to London. In full battle gear he rushed into the Acme office with his film. After the captions for his photographs were written, Brandt was in the jeep headed back to board another landing craft bound for France. His photographs were the first pictures of the invasion printed in American papers.

Jim McNamara was with a demolitions unit in the second wave of Marines to hit the beaches of Iwo Jima. Their bags of explosives were heavy and they threw them down into a ravine and fought their way inland. An officer spotted the same ravine and thought it would be the perfect place for the company latrine. Orders were shouted, planks were put over the ravine, and soon the johns were installed. The john was a crowd pleaser and for days that part of the campaign went well—until a Marine lit a cigarette while using the john and tossed it down the hole. McNamara heard the explosion over the gunfire. It was not a pretty sight.

One Sunday in 1943, as the photographers in Washington were making pictures of the first family leaving for church, the president scanned the group and yelled, "Where's Sammy?" Sammy Schulman of International News Service was one of Roosevelt's favorites. A photographer yelled back that Schulman had left town to cover the war in North Africa. A month later Schulman was in Casablanca covering the meeting between British Prime Minister Winston Churchill and Roosevelt. A smiling president greeted him with a loud, "Hi, Sammy!"

Vice presidents could add spice and life to a presidential administration. Most had been good friends of the photographers, too. One of the spiciest was John Nance Garner,

Vice President John Nance Garner with his friends the photographers in January 1941. Credit: WHNPA archives.

also known as "Cactus Jack," from Uvalde, Texas. Roosevelt's first vice president is best remembered for his remark about the value of the job: "The vice presidency is not worth a bucket of warm spit." (He actually said "piss.") Garner's friendship with photographers began when he was in the House of Representatives, and it continued into the White House. Photographers remembered that Garner always had a jug of liquor in the bottom drawer of his desk and was willing to share it.

Sometimes vice presidents were a bit too spicy and not such good friends. In July 1944 Vice President Henry Wallace was not in a good mood. There was a movement afoot by Democratic Party leaders to replace him as Roosevelt's running mate for the fall election with Senator Harry S. Truman or William O. Douglas, a Supreme Court justice. Roosevelt had told Wallace that he had confidence in him as vice president and that he would vote for him if he were a delegate to the convention. This was not the solid endorsement that Wallace needed to keep his job and everyone knew it.

On the day before the Democratic convention the possibility of a change in the candidate for vice president was a major story. Wallace lived in the Wardman Park Hotel (it is the Marriott Wardman today) and photographer Robert Woodsum of Acme News had been waiting in the lobby for five hours to make a photograph of Wallace. About five that afternoon the vice president entered the lobby and walked to the front desk to get his mail. Woodsum went over to Wallace and politely asked, "How about a picture, please?" In a loud voice the vice president said, "No, no, no!" and made for a stairway.

Woodsum went for the picture anyway, and at the flash of the bulb Wallace whirled around and yelled, "Give me that plate, give me that plate!" The vice president crouched down like a wrestler and suddenly lunged forward. The two men collided, sending the camera and flashbulbs flying. Both men were on the ground, the vice president on top of Woodsum. With a quick change of mood, Wallace backed off and helped Woodsum up. The photographer refused to give up the film, saying that it was his job to bring back a picture. A deal was struck: Woodsum would pull the slide on the camera, thereby destroying the picture, and the vice president would pose for a photograph.

Later that week at the party convention in Chicago, Truman was nominated vice president over Wallace. A couple of months later the outgoing vice president was asked about the photographic capabilities of Woodsum. "I'm sure of one thing, though," Wallace answered. "That man can rassle."

Separate from the press secretary was the travel office of the White House. Staffed with a group of "can do" individuals, the travel office solved the complicated problems that arose when moving the president, his entourage, the Secret Service, and the White House press across the United States or around the world. It made the arrangements for trains, planes, press rooms, and telephone lines. The members of the press or their organizations paid for all their own travel. The press did not and does not get a free ride to cover the president.

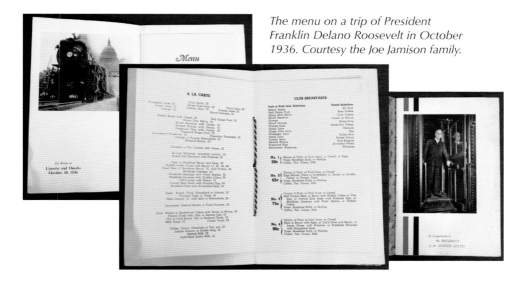

The menu on a trip of President Franklin Delano Roosevelt in October 1936. Courtesy the Joe Jamison family.

The sterling reputation of the travel office was built on the talents of Dewey Long, who headed the office during the Roosevelt administration. The president's train, named POTUS, consisted of baggage cars that transported Roosevelt's limousines, communications and security gear, and five coffee-green Pullman cars. Positioned at the end of the train was the president's special rail car, the *Ferdinand Magellan*, custom-made with steel plates and weighing 285,000 pounds.

Moving the Roosevelt train required travel over several train lines and building special ramps and loading facilities for the president. It took a man who could get the cooperation of railroad men up and down the line. Long and his second in charge, Edward "Jiggs" Fauver, made the impossible happen smoothly. The standard of first-class service for everyone involved a myriad of details to be addressed, but railroad men respected Long and his requests. Sometimes the trips were last-minute and often were made more difficult because some of Roosevelt's trips were kept secret from the public. Usually, the press had a pool of reporters on the train, but the trips were "off the record," so most of the reporters' work involved honing their poker-playing skills.

The Associated Press, United Press, and Acme photo departments were allowed to convert compartments on the presidential train into darkrooms to develop film and make prints between campaign stops. The six- to twelve-second exposure of a print in the enlarger was impossible because of the movement of the train. The problem was solved by putting a flash bulb in the enlarger, which exposed the paper in a fraction of a second—no movement and a sharp enlargement could be printed.

The *Ferdinand Magellan* carried Roosevelt to his summer White House in Warm Springs, Georgia, in March 1945. He suffered a fatal stroke there the following month. The president's funeral train included his special car, this time carrying first lady Eleanor Roosevelt. The *Ferdinand Magellan* remained in service throughout the Truman administration and off and on during most of the Eisenhower years until air travel became the standard. The president's car wound up in Miami's Gold Coast Railroad Museum. It was brought back to life a generation later to become the center piece of campaign swings for Ronald Reagan and George H.W. Bush.

Out of the Dog House

Harry S. Truman

Before he became vice president and then president, Harry Truman was a senator from Missouri. He got to know and like photographers Ed Alley of United Press, Frank Cancellare of Acme, and Henry Griffin of the Associated Press, the regulars on Capitol Hill. It was no surprise that this down-to-earth senator would enjoy the company of working men who showed no pretense. While all the other Senate committees closed their proceedings to photographers, Truman's committee investigating waste during wartime was open to cameras all the time.

AP photographer Max Desfor remembered going to Truman's Senate office in the Russell Building to pick him up and walk with him down to a committee room where the senator was to be one of the judges of the White House News Photographers Association's picture contest. Truman got halfway down a long hall and stopped. "I forgot something. Max, you wait right here," and the senator walked quickly back to his office. He returned with a brown paper bag and they went to the committee room where the contest photographs were laid out for the judging. Truman took a fifth of bourbon out of the brown pa-

Senator Truman at the judging of the WHNPA contest. Photo: Arthur Scott.

per bag, placed it on the table, and said, "Now we can begin."

Truman was sworn in as president upon Franklin D. Roosevelt's death in April 1945. At that time photographers at the White House had been working for years in a small, shed-like room that had previously been used by the executive mansion's florists. It was about six feet by twenty-five feet and ran along the White House outside of Roosevelt's swimming pool. (Today it would be just outside of the White House press briefing room.) The photographers would stand and wait for the president's visitors to come to the door. Stationed far from the print reporters in the press room, the photographers called it "the dog house."

Truman was taking a tour through the White House press room when he asked, "Where are the photographers?" Told that they were not allowed in the press room, he replied, "I want them in here."

The new president needed an official portrait. Instead of the traditional Harris & Ewing portraits used by past presidents, Truman opened the portrait session to many photographers—in fact, nearly one hundred cameramen and assistants showed up. There were so many that the group was divided into three parts. There was another photographic session, in January 1946, in which the first family—the president, first lady Bess Truman and their daughter, Margaret—posed for a group family photograph. More than forty photographers attended and the session lasted for almost an hour. Today, a photo

President Truman on his early morning walk. Credit: Harry S. Truman Library.

session with the president might last from ten to thirty seconds.

The daily Truman coverage began early—very early, photographer Arnie Sachs remembered, at times as early as five o'clock in the morning—with a two-mile walk around the city. There would be four or five reporters, the "stills" with their cameras, and a couple of Secret Service agents. Always along was agent Henry Nicholson, a tough, wide man who was the president's chief bodyguard. Truman usually walked out of the White House to Pennsylvania Avenue (it was open to traffic in those days), then down the avenue toward Capitol Hill. At different points, the president would make a right and walk toward the Mall, then up and around the Washington Monument, and return around the south side of the White House. With this president there was no taking a photograph or two and leaving. If you covered the morning walk, Truman made you cover the entire two miles. A club was formed named "The Truman Early Risers Walking Society."

On those early mornings Truman would pass the street cleaners hosing down the areas in front of the stores. They would say, "Good morning, Mr. President," and he would call back to them. Photographer George Tames noticed that the president would more

The photographers covering President Truman formed a small, very select club for the regulars joining President Truman on his walks.

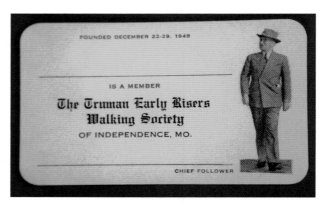

FOUNDED DECEMBER 22-29, 1948

IS A MEMBER

𝕿𝖍𝖊 𝕿𝖗𝖚𝖒𝖆𝖓 𝕰𝖆𝖗𝖑𝖞 𝕽𝖎𝖘𝖊𝖗𝖘
𝖂𝖆𝖑𝖐𝖎𝖓𝖌 𝕾𝖔𝖈𝖎𝖊𝖙𝖞

OF INDEPENDENCE, MO.

CHIEF FOLLOWER

than likely drop some of his personal letters right into the mailboxes during his outings. The staff would be angry at the Secret Service for letting the president mail the letters, but their complaints fell on deaf ears. Truman would do what he wanted to do.

Walking with Truman must have been a fun experience for the photographers—with one exception. Johnny Rouse, a very overweight man who worked for the AP, could not keep up with the president's brisk pace. Rouse would huff and puff along the two-mile walk, but Truman would stop and wait for him to catch up. In explaining his co-operation with the men and women carrying cameras, Truman once remarked, "Photographers have to make a living, too."

President Truman poses for the stillmen in the Oval Office, before a television address.

Truman bonded with the still photographers. He truly liked "the stills," and the feeling was mutual. Photographer Woody Wilson looked back on the Truman presidency when he was ninety-six and remarked, "He was the sort a guy you would like to be your uncle." A photographer for United Press, Jim Atherton, put it this way: "Covering Truman was like covering your best friend's father." Access to the president and his guests had never been better. The photographers would walk into the Oval Office —no reporters were allowed in— and at times were permitted to move the subjects around a little to make the best picture. When the senior photographer determined that they had enough, he would say, "Thank you, Mr. President." Truman would say, "Are you sure?" And inevitably a photographer would say, "Just one more."

The idea of "just one more" started right at the time that Truman took his oath of office. The photographers were all over the Cabinet Room trying to get a good picture of the historic moment. After the actual swearing-in, there was a plea from the stills for "just one more," so Roosevelt's press secretary, Jonathan Daniels, persuaded the new president to take the oath a second time.

A birthday cake from the photographers. Of course, there had to be a picture.

Later, Truman formed the "Just One More Club" and often told visitors about the club made up of his friends—and the fact that he was the president of the club. On many occasions Truman pointed to the photographers and said things like, "These are the hardest working men in town" or "These are the only fellows who can tell me what to do."

Truman's agreeable "just one more" attitude was not always in play. While the White House was undergoing a major renovation, the first family lived nearby at Blair House. On November 1, 1950, photographers Maurice Johnson of International News Photos and Bruce Hoertel, working for the *New York Times*, were walking to their cars on West Executive Avenue. Truman was to unveil a statue of the British military leader Sir John Dill later that afternoon at Arlington National Cemetery and they were heading there to cover the event. They heard gun shots and raced to Pennsylvania Avenue. Two men who supported Puerto Rico's independence had tried to assassinate the president. One of the men and a White House police officer died in an exchange of gunfire outside the residence.

Johnson made a picture of the mortally wounded guard. As he was putting the slide in and turning the 4x5 holder on his Speed Graphic he looked up and saw Truman leaning out of a second-story window of Blair House. Johnson was not fast enough because by the time he was ready to make his picture, the president was gone. No one made the picture, but it was an image that Johnson remembered for the rest of his life. He often mulled over how he could have made the photo that he had missed.

The president trusted his friends the photographers. He could make offhand comments to them without worrying that his remarks would show up in the newspaper the next day. Photographer George Tames remembers Truman talking about General Dwight D. Eisenhower and other military men and saying, "You know, George, a general without an army is just another G.I. named Ike." After Adlai Stevenson had been nominated as the Democratic candidate for president in 1952, Truman and Stevenson shared an elevator with three of the "stills men." The president pointed to the three and told Stevenson: "These are the best friends you'll ever have. They see everything, they know everything, and they say nothing."

Marion Carpenter became a favorite of Truman's during the three years she covered the White House for International News Photos, the only female photographer to travel routinely with the president. On a print of her photograph of the president walking toward the Washington Monument, Truman wrote: "It's good exercise if you keep it up, but not for high-heeled shoes, Miss Carpenter." She won several awards in the WHNPA contest and eventually became a freelance photographer.

Carpenter was noted for getting photographs of senators and congressmen who were reluctant to pose for other photographers. A columnist for the *Washington Post*, Tris Coffin, wrote in 1949 that she used her "persuasive feminine techniques" to obtain the photo sessions. While Coffin was eating lunch in the Senate press dining room, Carpenter came in, sat next to him, and ordered a bowl of bean soup, the large twenty-cent size. She turned to Coffin, announced, "Here's an exclusive for you," and dumped the bean soup on his head. She walked out of the dining room. Coffin paid for the soup. She told the *Post*, "I don't have to smile or tease anyone to get them to pose."

Henry Burroughs was one of the premier photographers for the Associated Press at the time. He recalled a sunny day in which Truman decided to visit the Pentagon to meet with Defense Secretary Louis Johnson. A small press pool accompanied the president on the ride to the Pentagon, where Johnson met Truman at the main entrance and escorted him to his office.

"The president told us that he would likely be forty-five minutes in a private session—no pictures," Burroughs said. "As all smart newsmen do when they have a chance, I headed for the men's room. I was standing at the urinal when shortly after the next urinal was occupied by none other than the president of the United States of America. I guess all smart presidents do the same thing as all smart newsmen." Flabbergasted, Burroughs managed a quiet "Hello, Mr. President." Truman looked at him and gave a good-natured smile. In a whimsical voice he told Burroughs, "This is the only place over here where anyone knows what they are doing."

Truman was a fan of the photographers. His secretary of state, Dean Acheson, was not. He looked down on all photographers— literally. One time Acheson was standing on a balcony with other diplomats and one of the photographers below shouted, "Just look over our heads, Mr. Secretary." Acheson replied, "We always do."

In the 1940's still photographers were not allowed to cover Senate hearings from gavel to gavel. Allowed in the hearing room for just a few minutes before the hearing started they had to make good photos quickly. Al Muto of International News Photos was a big man, not tall but large. He was the stereotypical image of the news photographer of the day: double-breasted suit, cigar clamped tightly in his mouth, and fedora with the press card stuck in the band. Muto was not known for his diplomatic skills. (On Queen Elizabeth's first visit to the United States, he wanted the monarch's attention and in a gruff voice yelled, "Hey, Queenie, look this way!")

A Senate hearing drew Muto and Acheson together. The photographers were leaning across the desk and urging Acheson to do something—a gesture, anything—for a photograph. Yet Acheson would not do anything worth making a picture. Muto began patting his Speed Graphic and telling the nation's top diplomat, "I make my living from this" and "My wife and my daughter get their bread and butter from this." Acheson just looked at Muto and finally said, "What do you wish me to do, take up a collection?"

The barb turned Muto silent, then angry. Photographer Frank Cancellare took his friend by the arm and left the hearing room with him. Muto was so angry that he talked about decking Acheson when he came out. "Al, take it easy," Cancellare said.

The traveling press leaves Fort Worth, Texas.

"There's no doubt in my mind that you can whip him physically. But please, don't trade wits!"

The travel office of the White House changed with the times but retained its reputation for serving the staff and the press. Truman traveled more and more by air while still logging plenty of miles on the *Ferdinand Magellan*, especially during the 1948 campaign. At one point, the Democratic National Committee ran out of money as Truman's train was heading north from Bonham, Texas. The press had paid their fares, but there was no money to pay for the other cars. The word got around that the train would be broken up and everyone would have to make their way back to Washington. Perle Mesta, the Washington social figure known as "the Hostess with the Mostest," was on the train and she wanted the train to travel on to her home state of Oklahoma. Mesta pulled out her checkbook and wrote a check for $5,000 and the Truman campaign train rolled on to Oklahoma City.

People often ended up running for the campaign train. A top aide to Truman at the time, Clark Clifford traveled with the president and on at least one occasion nearly missed the train as it left the station. Photographer George Tames was there, too, and witnessed Clifford's late arrival. Over the years, Clifford held various positions at the White House during a long career. Late in his life he was testifying at a House hearing on a banking scandal in which he was entangled. Tames was covering the hearing and recognized that it was an extremely stressful time for Clifford. During a break when the committee members went to the House chamber to vote, Tames leaned over and quietly reminded Clifford of those happy days with Truman—and the time nearly fifty years earlier when Clifford ran down the tracks to catch the campaign train, the photographers urging him on until he jumped on board. A most diplomatic smile came to the statesman's face and he said in a low voice, "And I still remember her name."

National Airlines was the first airline to fly a press charter. It was from Washington National Airport to Boca Chita, Florida. The president read his morning news thanks to a daily delivery of the New York and Washington newspapers courtesy of John Morris, the National Airlines vice president. The first overseas press charter flight, in October 1950, was a Pan American World Airways Stratocruiser that accompanied Truman from Washington to St. Louis, San Francisco, Hawaii and then Wake Island for a meeting between Truman and General Douglas MacArthur. Pan American was the logical choice for the charter because it had been serving Wake Island for years as

The photographers wait for President Truman on Wake Island. Photo: WHNPA.

a refueling stop for its sea planes. On the island, Truman rested for an hour or two at the quonset living quarters of the Pan American station manager.

Eight still and reel photographers accompanied Truman to Wake Island. The meeting between the commander in chief and the general overseeing the Korean War proved to be testy. MacArthur's plane had landed on Wake Island before Truman's plane, but the general kept the president waiting for forty minutes before he walked to the steps of the presidential plane, the *Independence*, to greet him. Truman was angry when he and MacArthur stepped into the little two-door sedan, the only civilian car on the island, that carried them to their meeting place. Al Muto of International News Photos made a prize-winning photograph through the rear window of the sedan as they left for their meeting. Truman and MacArthur were glaring at each other.

Secret Service agent Floyd M. Boring was the driver and could hear every word. As Boring recalled, Truman told MacArthur: "Listen, you know I'm president, and you're the general, you're working for me." That tone continued. "All right," Truman said, "you don't make any political decisions; I make the political decisions. You don't make any kind of a decision at all. Otherwise, I'm going to call you back, and get you out of there. If you make one more move, I'm going to get you out of there." The following year, Truman did just that, relieving MacArthur of command in Korea.

Truman cared about his friends. Frank Cancellare of Acme—everyone called him "Cancy"—and the AP's Henry "Griff" Griffin were often assigned to cover Truman. While they were competitors, Cancy and Griff enjoyed working on the same assignments and had gotten into trouble together all over the world. In those days wire service photographers often made their pictures from identical angles. Cancy was a small man and sometimes Griff would shoot right over him.

On one assignment, Cancy and Griff were walking backward down the aisle of the *Independence*, Truman's DC-6, and making pictures of the president, Griff shooting over the smaller Cancy. They came to the door and Cancy heard a whoosh and a thud.

President Truman's DC-6, The Independence. Photo: Abbie Rowe, National Archives.

The ground crew had not yet rolled the steps into place. There, lying fifteen feet below on the tarmac, lay Griff. His injuries resulted in a long convalescence at Walter Reed Hospital. Griff remembered

Truman calling him by phone and then coming out to see him a half-dozen times, one of the many private things the president did for others.

Truman vacationed at the Key West Naval Air Station eleven times while he was in office. These were major vacations; some lasted nearly a month. In contrast to the presidential vacations where the first family jumps from hiking, to fishing, to golf in a day, Truman limited his activities to an occasional fishing trip and the sport of poker. The photographers went along and loved every minute. The president stayed in the commandant's quarters and many of the photographers stayed in the Bachelor's Officers Quarters—Building 128. The press room was also in the BOQ. Truman would often walk into the BOQ just to check on how his boys were doing.

There were no credit cards back then and the photographers got their travel expenses in cash before they left Washington. Truman learned that INP photographer Al Muto was nearly broke. He and the other photographers were making their pictures when the president reached into his pocket. "Al," Truman said, "I hear you are running low on cash." He gave Muto a hundred-dollar bill and said, "Remember, this is a loan, not a gimme." Muto said, "I know, Mr. President"—then wired for more money as soon as he could.

Truman also appreciated the work of his friends. About three days after the president was the guest of honor at the opening of a White House News Photographers Association exhibit, he telephoned George Skadding, the association president. "George, there were so many people around me that I really didn't get a chance to look at the photographs," Truman said. "Can I come back and take a good look?" Skadding quickly made arrangements with the Statler Hotel (now the Capital Hilton) for a special viewing.

One Sunday morning all the photographers covering the White House were called to the South Lawn for an official photograph of the group. Truman posed with them, then took a Speed Graphic and made his own photo of the group and the White House. For its contest, the Association created a president's category in which only the president of the United States could enter. Truman entered—and won.

President Truman makes his award-winning photograph. Photo: WHNPA.

WHNPA President Eugene Abbott and Vice President Thomas Cravens Sr. give President Truman a watch at the last meeting of the "Just One More Club." Photo: WHNPA.

"Covering Mr. Truman was one of the most congenial experiences of my career," said *Washington Post* correspondent Edward T. Folliard, who had been at the White House since the Harding years and would stay through the Nixon administration. "I think this was because the Missouri gamecock, founder of the One More Club, thought of us reporters and photographers as members of his entourage, not interlopers or camp followers."

At the end of the Truman administration, the photographers had a dinner for the president—just Harry S. Truman and his Secret Service agents—and it was a great night. Truman even played the piano. At the end of the evening he thanked his friends, said good night, and left. The fellows were having a drink when they turned to see the president come back into the room. He ordered a toast and said, "I hereby declare the 'Just One More Club' dissolved."

GIVING THEM THE PICTURES THEY WANT

DWIGHT D. EISENHOWER

He was a five-star general of the Army, supreme commander of Allied Forces for the invasion of Europe in World War II, the supreme commander of NATO, Republican nominee for president—and Dwight D. Eisenhower almost met his maker at the hands of a news photographer. At least that was what photographer Henry Griffin thought.

In Boston on the eve of the 1952 election, Eisenhower was at a hotel making his final television appearance. Griffin, who had covered the general during the war, began adjusting a clock on a music stand behind the general to show just how late the candidate had been working that night. Griffin lost his grip on the heavy timepiece and it fell—*kerplop!*—right on Eisenhower's head. Thinking he had brained the general, Griffin dashed out of the room and headed down the hall looking for an exit. He glanced back and saw the cops closing in. Griffin thought, "Now I know he's dead."

The officers grabbed Griffin. Instead of arresting the photographer, one of the cops told him, "The general says nobody's going to make that picture until you get your shot."

President Eisenhower in the Oval Office. Credit: Abbie Rowe, National Archives.

Sometimes the best stories have a couple of endings. United Press International correspondent Helen Thomas told the story a different way: "The easel fell, putting a slight dent in Ike's bald head, and Griff beat a hasty retreat, never to be seen again for a few hours." Photographer Frank Cancellare remembered that Eisenhower, wanting to show that he was not angry, came looking for Griffin wearing a battle jacket and a small bandage on his head. When he found Griffin he bought the photographer a drink.

Eisenhower had been used to dealing with the press by the time he became president. A year before the 1952 campaign, shortly after he became supreme commander of the North Atlantic, he opened a joint meeting of Congress with a nod to the cameras: "I did not assume when I came up here that I would have also to play a role that was more fitting to Hollywood. But, as the vice president explained, it seems that the photographer has become often the arbiter of our fate and the dictator of our time and so I, like any other person, conform."

A painter, Eisenhower liked photographs and used them in his work on canvas. But he did not like dealing with cameras. Shortly after the war, he was given a Leica with filters and several lenses. He listened to a general showing him how to operate the Leica and then said, "Too damn much trouble." Eisenhower handed the Leica to an aide and told him if he wanted a picture, he would tell him what to take. One of the Leica pictures of a church in Bavaria was used for one of his paintings.

The best way to handle photographers, Eisenhower found over the years, was to give them the pictures that they wanted. There would be a wave, but only one. He smiled often enough, but he was sensitive about his earlobes, photographer George Tames remembered.

President Eisenhower with his Stereo Realist Camera at Washington National Airport.

"Ike had a funny thing about that smile," his press secretary, James Haggerty, remarked on one occasion. "It's elusive. To the still photographer, that is. The stills men who cover the president know what I mean. The smile pops up frequently enough, but how often do you really get a good picture of it? The timing is critical, but when you catch it just right you know you've got a bell ringer."

Hagerty was the key to the good relations that the photographers had with Eisenhower. "Ike hired the best

Press Secretary James Hagerty

Press Secretary Hagerty gives last-minute direction to the president before a televised address. Credit: Abbie Rowe, National Archives.

men and left them alone to do their job," said Jim Atherton, the White House photographer for UPI. The photographers thought Hagerty was the best. He had been a reporter for the *New York Times* and knew what made a picture. As Arnold Sachs remembered: "You always knew where you stood with Jim. He was straight with the photographers."

Hagerty paid attention to the photographers. "Listen, Mr. Hagerty," one cameraman said as he pointed to his Speed Graphic, "one picture on this can tell the story better than ten thousand words that those pencil boys can write." Sometimes he did not enjoy the conversations, but Haggerty would listen.

And he would look out for them. One day he came up to the photographers and said, "Be sure to be here on Thursday." Sure enough, they were invited up to the White House dining room for a lunch of "cluckers," small birds, probably doves, that had been prepared by Eisenhower's chef. The president had shot them while on a hunting trip with an Alabama congressman.

Dave Wiegman, an NBC cameraman, recalled one of the first press pools on Eisenhower's plane, the *Columbine*. Hagerty came back to the press section and said, "The president wants to talk." They went forward to where Eisenhower was sitting. "The reason I wanted to talk," the president said, "is that there is something I wanted you to try." He handed Wiegman and the others a new Metracal cookie, the first of the high-protein cookies. "How's that taste?" Eisenhower asked. "I think this will be good for you."

"Ike would make out like he didn't know you, but he really did," remembered Arnold Sachs. Of course, Henry Griffin was one of his favorites. Frank Jurkoski of INP was another. The Cravens, Tom Sr.

and Tom Jr., were Eisenhower's favorites among the newsreel photographers. The two Irishmen always had a wisecrack to share with Eisenhower. The president would look around and if one of the Cravens was missing, he would ask, "Where's Junior?" or "Where's Senior?"

President Eisenhower with Thomas Craven Senior and Junior.

Eisenhower's darker moods were infamous. As did a lot of network correspondents, John Cochran started his career as a radio reporter. On one of his first days covering the White House, he was concerned that he might not have the right connection to the "mult" box where everyone could receive the sound from the president's microphone. Cochran went to the Rose Garden well before the event and was working with his wires when Eisenhower came walking down the colonnade. The president stopped and asked in sort of a harsh tone: "What are you doing here? Don't you know reporters aren't supposed to be in this area?" Cochran apologized and went back to the press room. Later, he described the exchange to Hagerty. "Did he have his brown suit on?" Hagerty asked. Cochran thought for a moment and said, "Well, yes, he did." Hagerty said: "That explains it. Ike is always in a bad mood when he has his brown suit on."

The Cold War with the Soviet Union marked the Eisenhower years. Children were hiding under their desks or along the school hallways in practice for a possible atomic blast. At noon on June 15, 1955, Operation Alert began. Soviet bombers were heading to the United States. About 15,000 federal workers were taken to air raid shelters out of Washington. Eisenhower was rushed to a secret location in the Virginia mountains where he signed a presidential proclamation declaring the United States under martial law. It was all just a drill, of course.

Part of the emergency plan, if ever actually undertaken, was to have a single still photographer accompany the presidential party to the bomb shelter. *Life* magazine wanted its staffer to be that photographer. The weekly magazine did not staff the White House every day, but it assigned a photographer to the White House to become one of the regulars. Still, the *Life* photographer was not the one designated to go to the shelter. In the bottom of one of the many briefcases carried by presidential military aides, there might be a "doomsday" contingency plan—and it might include a news photographer.

WHY THEY MADE THAT PICTURE

JOHN F. KENNEDY

The new tools and trends in news photography came together as the sixties began. High-speed films and 35mm cameras allowed the intimate coverage of everyday activities. Pictures could be made without posing the subjects and freezing the action with a flash. The decisive moment and meaningful reportage replaced the clichés of the past. A new group of educated, more sophisticated photographers wanted to tell stories with their pictures.

John F. Kennedy was the perfect presidential candidate for this new era. He was a great subject for photographs—and he knew it. By allowing ac-

Jacques Lowe photographing President Kennedy in the Rose Garden. Photo: Abbie Rowe, National Archives.

President Kennedy meets with a delegation of Indian chiefs in the Rose Garden. Photo: Abbie Rowe, National Archives.

cess to a few trusted photographers Kennedy ensured photographic coverage that showed the youthful, confident leader he wanted the voters to see. He had a good eye for photographs, appreciating great pictures and disliking corny poses and anything that would make him look awkward. He disliked hats that were given to him to wear during the 1960 campaign. A cowboy hat would be quickly handed off to an aide. During one event an American Indian headdress came close to the top of his head. He asked, "They're not going to give me a bunch of feathers to wear, are they?"

The inauguration was a perennial contest to see which wire service could deliver the first photograph of the new president taking the oath of office. In January 1961, Gary Haynes of United Press International came up with an unusual way of beating the Associated Press. He installed a 4x5 "Big Bertha"—a modified RB Super D Graflex usually used for sporting events—on a sturdy tripod on the elevated photographers' stand directly in front of where Kennedy would take the oath. Using Polaroid film, Haynes planned to make a picture as soon as Kennedy raised one hand and put the other on the Bible.

"We had arranged for power and two phone lines up to the stand and early that morning," he remembered. "I hooked up one of UPI's custom transmitters we had retrofitted to take 4x5 prints instead of the usual UPI standard 7x9." When Kennedy raised his hand, Haynes made the first picture and put it in his shirt as it developed. He had already written a caption on a label to be stuck on the photo.

"The startled Associated Press photographer watched when I put the photo on the drum at my feet while I shot a second picture," Haynes said. "Four minutes later the first photo had been transmitted to U.S. and Europe. The second print went to Asia, I recall, and both had been transmitted almost before JFK finished the oath of office."

Shortly after the inauguration the president asked an old friend, General Chester V. Clifton, to be his military aide. Clifton also had a friend, Captain Cecil Stoughton, a photographer in the Army Signal Corps. Soon Stoughton was assigned to the White House. His pictures were more straightforward, for the historical record. The Kennedys liked having Stoughton around—he was great with the children—but they also wanted other looks at the presidency by photojournalists.

Not unlike Franklin D. Roosevelt, Kennedy had his rules and demanded loyalty from the news photographers to whom he granted access. This rule was simple enough: No pictures were to be taken of Kennedy wearing eyeglasses. One day photographer George Tames was called into the Oval Office. Immediately the president jumped up and handed Tames a copy of the *New York Times Magazine*. It was opened to a page with a picture of Kennedy with eyeglasses on the top of his head. "Why did you publish a picture of me like this?" the president asked. Tames pointed out that he did not take the picture; it had been sold to the *Times* by Jacques Lowe, a freelance photographer who had been granted a great deal of access to the Kennedys. The president picked up the phone and called his press secretary, Pierre Salinger, into the office. He ordered Salinger to tell Lowe that he was no longer granted access. When Salinger left, the president told Tames, "Jacques Lowe shit the nest and he's got to go."

In his first month in office, Kennedy allowed Tames to do a "day in the life of the president" story. The Kennedy staff called it a "Day in the Closet" and every photographer wanted to have his day. Tames did not actually stand in the closet. He spent his time in the Oval Office in a small chair that he placed near the door to the Cabinet Room. He had to be quiet—doing anything without talking was hard for him—while making a few unposed photographs of Kennedy going about his work.

Every good photographer knows if a subject does something once, there is a very good chance that he or she will do it again. Tames had photographed Kennedy in his Senate office on Capitol Hill and knew that Kennedy's back gave him a great deal of pain. Kennedy had a habit of supporting himself while reading by leaning on his desk or on a window sill. In the Oval Office for the day, Tames waited for such a moment.

It happened in the perfect location. Kennedy was facing the three Oval Office windows overlooking the South Lawn and leaned over in just the perfect spot in the middle of the windows. The president, looking down at some papers, appeared in silhouette. Tames got up from his chair, walked over, and made the picture. As Tames moved a little closer and to the side for another view he noticed that Kennedy was reading the *New York Times* editorial page, which featured its prize-winning columnist Arthur Krock. The president heard the camera clicking, looked up, and said, "I wonder where Mr. Krock gets all the crap he puts in this horseshit column of his."

The picture, "The Loneliest Job in the World," was one of the most famous images of the Kennedy years. The original negative went missing shortly after the photograph was made. Fortunately the *New*

Photo: George Tames, The New York Times, Redux.

York Times had made an excellent copy negative. Some twenty-five years later, after Tames had retired, James Wallace of the Smithsonian Institution Museum of American History had a researcher work with Tames as they went through his photographs at his home. The researcher found some scraps of paper and showed Tames a tiny note saying "LJ SD" and asked if it meant anything. Tames immediately ran up the stairs to his bedroom and went to the top drawer of his dresser. He rummaged through his socks and came up with an envelope. Inside was the missing negative. Tames had wanted to put the negative someplace safe. He had made a tiny note to remind himself. "LJ SD" meant "Loneliest Job Sock Drawer."

First lady Jacqueline Kennedy had a love-hate relationship with photography. In 1951, two years before she married a young senator from Massachusetts, she took over the job as the "Inquiring Photographer" at the *Washington Herald* when Lou Hollis left town to cover the Korean War. The column was comprised of answers to questions asked to a Washington personality and a photographic portrait of the person being interviewed. Then twenty-two years old, Jacqueline Bouvier knew nothing about the developing and printing of the pictures that she had to submit to her editors. In fact, she really did not like working in the darkroom. Joe Heiberger, a photographer for the *Herald* and later for the *Washington Post*, helped her learn the art of developing film and making prints. She often asked Heiberger to do her darkroom work and he did it willingly. Years later when Heiberger covered her as first lady, she did not acknowledge him, and that irritated Heiberger.

Part of Mrs. Kennedy's lack of acknowledgement of Heiberger could have been because of an ongoing battle that she had with newspaper photographers. One skirmish could have been a mistake. When Arnie Sachs was coming back to the *Washington Star*, he saw a crowd of tourists looking through the fence on the South Lawn. He stopped his car right on E Street, which ran along the South Lawn fence. The street was open to vehicular traffic at that time and a news photographer could actually make pictures without being bothered by police. Sachs got out of his car and went over to see what everyone was watching. The Kennedys' daughter, Caroline, was riding her pony, Macaroni. Sachs made a picture, went in to the *Star* and developed the film. While he was making the prints, the assignment editor came in with another assignment. Sachs told the editor about the picture and went off to do the assignment.

When Sachs returned, the same editor was at the door telling him the senior editors wanted to see him immediately. "Why did you make that picture?" one of them demanded. Sachs did not know that the Kennedys had an agreement with the wires not to make pictures of activities of Caroline and her younger brother, John. The *Star*, an evening paper at that time, had just printed the picture on page one and press secretary Pierre Salinger was angry. He had already received a note from the first lady: "I thought that you had made an arrangement with the fotogs not to take pictures of the children playing at the White House. They have had all the pictures of Macaroni they need. I want no more—I mean this—and if you are firm and will take the time, you can stop it. So please do. That is what a press secretary is for—to help the press yes—but also to protect us."

Kennedy himself made an end run around his wife's rules about photographing their children. His public ratings were at a low in the fall of 1963 and he was afraid that they would drop to a much lower level as a result of Senate hearings looking into the financial and personal activities of Bobby Baker, the recently resigned secretary for the Senate majority leader. Investigators would no doubt ask about a Baker friend, Elly Rometsch, a German woman later suspected of being a spy as well as a paramour of the president. Kennedy knew that nothing raised his ratings more than pictures of him with Caroline and John. He waited until Mrs. Kennedy was scheduled to be out of town and called Stanley Tretick, a news photographer he could trust.

Tretick had been a photographer for United Press International, and he was good. He had covered the Korean War and was a regular White House News Photographers Association prizewinner. He was aggressive and he was always right up front. He loved to razz the other photographers about his exclusives. In turn, the photographers were always mimicking his Brooklyn nasal accent, but he took it in stride. When Tretick covered the Kennedy campaign for UPI, the candidate liked him and gave him a few exclusives. It was not long before he joined the staff of *Look* magazine to cover the White House. For months he had been pushing to do a story on the president and his son.

Stanley Tretick photographing President Kennedy as he waves farewell to a visiting head of state. Photo: Abbie Rowe, National Archives.

When Kennedy called, he told Tretick, "Things get kind of sticky around here when Mrs. Kennedy is around, but Mrs. Kennedy is away." Tretick rushed to the White House with his two Nikon F's, then spent a week doing the story. One of the pictures was of two-year-old John playing under the Oval Office desk while Kennedy was at work. His picture showing the president with John was on the cover of the December 3, 1963, issue of *Look*, which featured Tretick's exclusive picture story. Released well ahead of its issue date, as was the custom of the weekly magazines, the magazine was already on newsstands when the president and the first lady traveled to Dallas, Texas, on November 22, 1963.

Henry Burroughs of the Associated Press and Frank Cancellare of United Press International were not happy with the motorcade arrangement at Love Field, the Dallas airport. The pool photographers' convertible was six cars back of the *Queen Mary*, the large black car with the wide running boards that carried the Secret Service. Normally the photographers' pool car was one or two cars back, but that day additional cars carrying the VIPs had been added to the motorcade. There was nothing to be done so Burroughs and Cancellare made a few pictures of Kennedy working the crowd at the airport and headed to their car for the ride into the city.

Burroughs remembered hearing the first shot as the motorcade passed through Dealey Plaza. "Must be a Texas salute," someone in the car remarked. Burroughs said, "Then we heard

The presidential limousine in Dallas on November 22, 1963. Photo: Warren Commission Report.

an ominous succession of shots." The motorcade came to a halt, but the Kennedy limousine and the Secret Service follow-up car were traveling away from the scene at great speed. The official White House photographer, Captain Cecil Stoughton, pulled out his White House credentials and ordered the driver to speed toward the Dallas Trade Mart, the building where Kennedy was scheduled to speak at a luncheon. The pool car stopped again as people ran to a grassy knoll in the plaza, and Cancellare jumped out of the pool car to make pictures. Tom Craven Jr. of CBS News jumped out of the television pool convertible behind the still pool car. The motorcade began to move.

A Secret Service agent climbed into the stills car. It was Lem Johns, the only Kennedy detail agent to rush up the knoll. They were moving, but they had no idea where they should go. The car stopped and Johns got out and talked to a motorcycle policeman, who used his radio to find out where the president's car was headed. Johns jumped on the back of the officer's three-wheel motorcycle and raced to Parkland Hospital, the pool car following.

Joe Laird, a handsome, easygoing man, was the best sports photographer at the *Dallas Morning News*. One of his success secrets was his Novaflex, a push pull telephoto lens that had a rifle stock for stability. It was an unfortunate choice of equipment to use on November 22 in Dallas. Laird saw his old friend Lyndon Johnson, then the vice president, getting into a car at Parkland Hospital. When he approached Johnson with his Novaflex, Johnson cowered below the window level of the car. Laird might have known just half of the story because Secret Service agent Rufus Youngblood was telling Johnson to get down at that exact moment.

As the official photographer for the Kennedy White House, Captain Cecil Stoughton had made many important photographs, but he was about to make the picture of his life and he was sweating. Sure, the body heat of the twenty-six people crammed in the stateroom of Air Force One was a factor, but that was not why Stoughton's shirt and sports coat were turning damp. His Swedish-made Hasselblad Superwide was not user-friendly. In addition to handling a fussy camera, he was working with a lens that he had just received. It had an extremely wide field of view, which he was thankful to have in the crowded plane. The Metz 514 strobe he carried was reliable, but it was connected to the camera by an x-sync cord that could short out at any time.

Stoughton was right to be worried. Everyone was in place for the swearing-in of Lyndon B. Johnson as the thirty-sixth president. Lady Bird Johnson stood to his right and Mrs. Kennedy to his left. As District Court Judge Sarah T. Hughes administered the oath of of-

Cecil Stoughton's photograph of Vice President Lyndon Baines Johnson taking the presidential oath of office on Air Force One in Dallas, Texas.

fice, Stoughton's Hasselblad failed. Actually, the camera itself worked, but the flash did not fire. Stoughton looked down, pushed the x-sync cord into the connection, and tried again. Thank God, it worked.

Stoughton had two cameras with him, both loaded with black-and-white film (Kodak Tri-X). His flash was on the Hasselblad. He directed the head of the Metz flash upward and bounced the light off the ceiling of Air Force One. It was a low ceiling and he was able to shoot at f/16, which gave him a tremendous depth of field. During the seventeen-second oath he shot a couple of frames with the flash and switched to his 35mm camera to backstop his efforts with available light photographs. In this stressful situation the speed of 1/60 of a second and an aperture of f/4 was just workable with a steady hand. Between the flash and available light pictures, Stoughton made twelve or thirteen frames.

With the Air Force One engines revving up, Stoughton rushed down the steps and over to Hank Burroughs of the AP and Frank Cancellare of UPI. He decided to stay with the film and not fly back to Washington. To decide which wire service would handle the film, they flipped a nickel and Burroughs won. Stoughton got a police car to drive all three photographers to the AP's Dallas photo office, which was in the *Dallas Morning News* building. Although there was little that he could do, Stoughton stayed with the film as it was developed. When the film came out of the hypo, then washed and held up to the light, Stoughton started to breathe again—they were in focus and the exposure was right on.

The photographers selected the best frame and made two prints, one for AP and one for UPI. It was very important that the transmissions of the photos to AP and UPI members start at the same time. One wet print was handed to a UPI motorcycle courier to rush to the UPI office in the *Dallas Times Herald*. Everyone waited. There was a great deal of pressure on Burroughs from the top AP management in New York to send the picture. The picture was on the transmission drum and the caption was written, but Burroughs waited. Finally the call came from Cancellare at the UPI bureau. At that point Stoughton gave a countdown—*three, two, one*—and both wire services rolled the historic picture of Johnson taking the oath of office. Stoughton watched over his negatives as they dried and placed them in an envelope, which he put in his pocket, and carried them back to the Services Lab in Washington. The lab was located in Foggy Bottom where the John F. Kennedy Center for the Performing Arts stands today.

Photographs made by George Tames about the same time would never be seen by anyone. On that sleepy Friday, Tames was at the Capitol. The news of Kennedy's assassination circulated like a lightning bolt and in the turmoil Tames went into the balcony of the United States Senate. No photographs were ever allowed to be made from the balcony, but Tames thought that an exception might be made at this historic moment. Along with Jim Atherton of UPI, Tames made pictures of senators reacting to the tragic news, consoling each other, pointing, and shouting. As Atherton remembered, Tames had second thoughts about making the pictures and breaking the rules. He told the Capitol Hill police about his pictures, thinking that the officers would agree that the historic moment should be covered. He was wrong—the police took his film and a part of history was lost forever.

The most remembered photograph from Kennedy's funeral was the image of his son saluting the caisson bearing the casket as it left St. Matthew's Cathedral in Washington to travel to Arlington National Cemetery. Historian William Manchester described John's salute: "His elbow was cocked at precisely the right angle, his hand was touching his shock of hair, and his left arm was rigidly at his side, his shoulders squared and his chin in. It was heart-wrenching."

The story behind the salute began weeks earlier. Kennedy was scheduled to lay a wreath at the Tomb of the Unknown Soldier on Veterans Day and decided to take his son along. The young boy was fascinated with military equipment: guns, uniforms, and especially helicopters. Mrs. Kennedy thought that it would be nice if John would salute at the event. At first he used his left hand; the salute definitely needed practice. Bob Foster, the Secret Service agent in charge of the children's protection, was asked to help and he practiced saluting with John. Veterans Day came and John was everywhere. On that day he was fascinated with the cameras. Photographer Fred Ward remembered kneeling, shooting from a low angle to get John and the large men behind him in the same picture. The child was tugging at the cameras around Ward's neck—he wanted to take pictures, too. Ward took one off, handed it to John, and prayed that his Leica M 2 would not be dropped on the hard marble of the cemetery steps.

Two weeks later, on his third birthday, John sat in a pew at St. Matthew's Cathedral during his father's funeral Mass. He did not understand where he was and began to fidget. Secret Service agent Bob Foster thought the little boy had had enough of the ceremony and carried him back to a holding room. A Marine colonel came into the room and Foster said, "Why don't you give the colonel a salute?" The colonel bent down and told John that the salute was to be made with his right hand and gently straightened his hand to a perfect salute. They practiced standing at attention and saluting a number of times.

When the service was completed John joined his mother and sister and walked down the steps of St. Matthew's to wait for the president's casket to be loaded on the caisson. John had a pamphlet that Foster had given him to draw on, but Mrs. Kennedy bent over, took the pamphlet, and whispered something in her son's ear. Just as the casket was passing, John came to attention and gave a salute that made the colonel proud.

UPI photographer Stan Stearns had been one of the three photographers who had walked with the funeral entourage from the White House to St. Matthew's. After the service Stearns was to walk with the entourage to Arlington Cemetery. He squeezed in next to Frank Cancellare, who was in the "fixed position" with hundreds of media across Rhode Island Avenue. There was no sense in two UPI photographers side by side shooting the same thing so Stearns and Cancellare decided that Cancellare would make the overall pictures and the color and Stearns would make the pictures from a long lens, 200mm at that time.

At the peak of John's salute, Stearns triggered the shutter of his Nikon F—and knew he had just made the best picture of his life. After the caisson rolled away, Stearns started asking the other photographers if they got the salute picture. Their reaction was the same: "What are you talking about?" Stearns realized that he not only had the picture but it could be an exclusive.

There was one major problem: The image of John was only 1/8 of the 35mm frame. When "Big John" Steinberger, the motorcycle courier, came for the film, Stearns said he was carrying this roll to the UPI bureau personally. He arrived at the bureau to find George Gaylin, the head of the bureau, livid. "Why didn't you go on the final half of the procession?" Gaylin yelled. Stearns replied that he had the picture of the funeral. All of the top management of UPI pictures had come to Washington for

Stan Stearns and President Johnson and the award-winning photo of John's salute. Photo: Stan Stearns.

the funeral and the head of UPI pictures grabbed Stearns by his tie and said, "You had better have the picture or you are fired." Stearns patted his pocket with the roll of Tri-X and said, "It's right here." In the wire service culture of "a deadline every minute," Stearns told his bosses the unthinkable: "You will have to wait to see this picture."

Stearns walked out of the UPI bureau and down to Penn Camera where he purchased a box of Microdol X developer. He knew that the film developer at UPI—Decktol and D 76, a mixture that would develop film quickly but not properly—would make the grain in the small image of John look like golf balls. He needed a fine grain developer. As he developed the film, Stearns could hear the men outside the dark room grumbling. He unrolled the film from the developing tank reel and found that the one frame was right on. He dried the negative, put it in a sleeve and handed it to Gaylin. The boss declared: "Holy shit! He does have the picture of the funeral!" The next morning papers across the nation agreed, putting John's salute on their front pages.

The story of John's salute was not over. For decades a North Carolina photographer, Joe O'Donnell, claimed to be the photographer who made the salute photograph and many other iconic pictures. O'Donnell was a folk hero in his area, selling his prints and lecturing about his famous work. It was not until his death in 2007 and a *New York Times* obituary that O'Donnell's ruse was discovered. Everyone in the picture business knew the salute photograph and knew that Stan Stearns was the man who had made it. Four weeks later the *Times* published a story about O'Donnell's erroneous claim—and others regarding other photographs—and issued a correction to set the record straight.

THAT WAS JUST LBJ

LYNDON B. JOHNSON

As do most representatives and senators, Lyndon Baines Johnson knew if there was a photographer in the room. A creature of Capitol Hill who also understood the power of publicity, he would direct his movements to the camera. He also knew what he wanted to look like in a picture because he had been trained by professionals.

Johnson was a congressman when the Japanese attacked Hawaii's Pearl Harbor in 1941. A lieutenant commander in the Naval Reserve at the time, Johnson wanted to go to war but on his own terms, so he embarked on a secret mission. When someone called his office and asked for the congressman, the caller was told that his location could not be given "because of military secrecy." Actually, he was in California on an inspection trip of Naval facilities while he waited for the Department of the Navy to grant him the job in Washington that he wanted. Lieutenant Commander Johnson liked Hollywood as his California operations base and his friend Edwin L. Weisl Sr., counsel for Paramount Pictures, was a great help in "arranging things." Johnson had never been pleased with his publicity photographs so long sessions with a Hollywood photographer were arranged. He studied the photographs made of him. He knew what he liked and set about to do something to eliminate the making of pictures that he did not like.

Long before he became president upon John F. Kennedy's death in 1963, Johnson knew what he wanted from the photographers. He

President Johnson's good side. Photo: Dennis Brack.

thought his best side was his left side, and advancemen were sure to place the photographers on the left side of the presidential podium. He was concerned about the deep shadows on his face caused by the television lights in the East Room of the White House. For press conferences a canopy was placed around the podium to allow the lights to be lowered for a flat, more pleasing light.

This president had a few problems with the photographers. He did not like their flashes, but he could do little about that if he wanted his picture in the papers. He thought the noise of the Nikon motor drives was distracting during his press conferences, and there was something that he could do about that. The photographers would be allowed only one minute at the beginning of the press conferences to make their pictures. Removing the photographers would be even more distracting than the noise of their camera shutters, so they were to stay in place until the conclusion of the press conference.

The assistant press secretary, Joe Laitin, stood in the front of the room and was under orders to enforce the "no shooting" rule which, of course, the photographers were going to break. A photographer on one side of the room would ease off a frame. Laitin would point his pencil at the offender with a scowl that said "bad photographer, bad photographer," then a photographer on the other side of the room would shoot a picture. Laitin would turn and point his

President Johnson during a White House East Room event. Photo: Abbie Rowe, National Archives.

pencil, another frame with another Laitin point-and-scowl. It looked like Laitin was directing an orchestra. The photographers knew that Laitin was going to face Johnson's wrath and limited their frames.

Joe Laitin was one of the best of the thousands of "flacks" who passed through Washington. He had some impressive journalistic credentials. He began his career as a United Press reporter. Later, as a reporter for Reuters, he covered the surrender of Japan on the battleship *Missouri*, the Nuremburg trials of Nazi war criminals, and the atomic tests on Bikini Atoll. (I remember Laitin talking about his days as a freelance writer-producer in Hollywood.) He appreciated just how much photographs helped in selling stories to the magazine.

Laitin was also a survivor. Take a look at the jobs he had in Washington: He came to town to work for Kennedy's budget director, then went to the White House as assistant press secretary, back to the Bureau of the Budget, then on to the Pentagon as assistant secretary of defense for public affairs. In 1975 he went to the press office of the Federal Aviation Agency and in 1977 to the Treasury Department as assistant secretary of the treasury for public affairs. Laitin survived because he dealt honestly and somewhat creatively with the reporters and photographers who worked in Washington. They knew that he was a public relations man, knew which side he was on, and knew that he could be of help. He was worth their time. There were only a few who earned that trust and Laitin was on the top of the list.

Another change was taking place during the Johnson years. More women were joining men in making pictures at the White House and elsewhere in Washington. In 1966, Margaret Thomas became the first female photographer at the *Washington Post*. The photo director, Dick Darcy, asked Thomas to begin work in the photo department as his secretary for a few months. His reason? As Thomas recalled, "so the male photographers could get used to a woman's presence."

When Johnson liked or disliked a picture he let the photographer know—in person. In 1964, the president and one of his beagles were with a group of visitors to the White House. Johnson lifted the dog by his ears. Associated Press photographer Charles Gory made the picture, which appeared in papers across the country and upset untold numbers of dog lovers. The next day, Gory got a lecture from the president. "Charlie, why did you take a picture like that?" Johnson asked. "That picture got me in a heap of trouble. Don't ever take a picture like that again!" Gory just smiled and with his deep, leprechaun-like voice said, "Oh no, Mr. President." Anyone who knew Gory knew he would make the same picture again in a heartbeat.

A presidential admonishment was no problem for Gory. He walked with a bit of a stoop when he covered the White House, the product of a lifetime of brave actions in dangerous places to make his pictures. He was cited for his "heroic and meritorious achievement" for his rescue efforts during a fire on a Navy ship in the Pacific in World War II.

Standing up to Johnson was the only way to gain his respect. One day Jim Atherton, a photographer for United Press International, was walking along the White House colonnade back to the press room. He felt two large hands on his shoulders and recognized the president's Texas drawl as he asked, "Jim, did you make any bad pictures of me today?" Atherton quickly replied, "No, but I'm still trying."

If Johnson liked a picture he let you know. Bryon Schumaker worked for the *Washington Star* and made a wonderful picture of Senate Minority Leader Everett Dirksen. The next day Schumaker was in the *Star* darkroom when he heard a yell. "Bryon, you got a call." He lingered and there was another more urgent yell. "Bryon, you've got to take this call right now!" He picked up the phone and heard Johnson's voice. The president had called to tell Schumaker how much he liked the Dirksen portrait and to ask him for a print.

Gathered in the front yard of Bethesda Naval Hospital, the photographers were unsure how Johnson would react to having his picture made. The president was recovering from a gall bladder operation and liked to spend time sunning himself at the hospital's helipad. Deck chairs and reclining lounges were placed around the large, round expanse of white cement. It was just like a swimming pool, but there was no pool.

A group of reporters and photographers—Charlie Tasnadi of the AP, Frank Cancellare of UPI, Gene Forte of Consolidated, and myself, working for *Time*—were taken out to the helipad to spend some time with the president. Someone asked a question about his health, and the president pulled back his sports coat, raised his shirt and

President Johnson and his scar. Photo: Dennis Brack.

gestured to his scar. There was complete silence for a second as the photographers considered what Johnson might do after the cameras started to work. With this president you never knew. Tasnadi, Forte, and I were in the right place to make the picture. Cancellare was on the wrong side but moving quickly. Tasnadi made the first frame and our Nikon motor drives followed. His picture was the best.

Years later I was photographing Jack Valenti, a top aide to Johnson at the time of the gall bladder operation, and I asked him about that afternoon and the scar picture. Valenti said that the president wanted us to make that picture because he was afraid that many people thought he had cancer and that his illness was much more serious. By showing his scar, he was trying to put those rumors to rest.

Four words often explained why Johnson would do things: That was just LBJ. He was a man who did what he wanted to do and others would have to make their adjustments. Photographer Frank Johnston, working for UPI, had just missed the president in Austin, Texas, but he knew the road the president was taking. Johnston put the pedal to the metal trying to catch up. Just as he came up over a

Jack Valenti. Photo: Dennis Brack.

hill he faced the last car of the presidential motorcade. He braked and stopped within inches of the last car. Then he looked over and saw Johnson by the roadside calmly answering nature's call—with everyone in the motorcade watching. While the president was calm, Secret Service agent Lem Johns was not. He slammed his hand on the hood of the photographer's car and declared, "If you ever come up on us like that again, I'll pull your pass."

Frank Johnston recalled another "That was LBJ" moment with a Secret Service agent. Johnson and an agent were at the president's ranch in Texas when they came upon a huge jackrabbit. They got very close to the rabbit and Johnson told the agent, "Shoot that thing." The agent demurred, saying something like, "Well, Mr. President, I don't think that's such a good idea." Johnson replied, "I am the president of the United States and I order you to shoot that rabbit." The agent drew his firearm and shot the rabbit. You can imagine the radio traffic on the Secret Service radio network.

When photographer George Tames drove up to the ranch house one time, Johnson came out and was pleased to see him. "I want you to take a picture of me and my new bull," the president told him. They hopped into Johnson's white Lincoln Continental and raced across the ranch as the Secret Service tried to keep up. After they found the bull, Tames walked to the front of the large prize winner and waited for the president. "George," the president said, "come back here." He found the president squatting next to the parts of the bull that he thought were most important. Johnson said, "I didn't pay all of that money for this bull's pretty face." Later that day, the president admonished Tames not to show the photos to "those folks at the *New York Times.*" Only a very few people have seen them.

At the White House, Roddey Mims, a photographer for UPI, was sitting on one of the leather couches in the press lobby when someone from the press office yelled, "Roddey, the president wants you

right now!" He grabbed his Rolliflex and Heiland Strobe and hurried to the elevator to the private residence, located on the second floor of the White House. When he went through the bedroom Mims saw the president of the United States standing and shaving—stark naked. Johnson turned and growled, "Roddey, what are you doing here?" Mims answered, "You called for a photographer." Johnson replied, "Damn it, I called for a stenographer, not a photographer!"

Roddey Mims. Photo: Dick Van Nostrand.

A wonderful unpublished picture by the official White House photographer at the time, Yoichi Okamoto, showed the top presidential advisers standing in a tiny hallway, taking notes and looking intently around the corner. Johnson was obviously sitting on the john and issuing orders. That was just LBJ.

Johnson had little regard for the people whose lives revolved around him. For example, no one knew whether he would travel to his ranch for the weekend. Every week Secret Service agents, staff, and the White House press would have their bags packed and the travel office would have a press plane standing by. Early Friday afternoon, Johnson would let his staff know and the travel arrangements would fall into place. It could be as quick as the time when the president stuck his head into press secretary George Reedy's office and said, "If you're going to Texas with me, you'd better come along," and headed to Marine One for the helicopter ride to his plane. There could be no weekend plans for anyone. Of course, this spread out to the family members of the staff, press, and Secret Service—another factor that created tension and stress in the White House.

Since the Roosevelt administration the people in the White House travel office had carried on the Dewey Long tradition of making the impossible happen. Even before Johnson became president, last-minute presidential trips to remote locations were part of the job. They were experts at staying calm under stressful conditions. They had a talent for listening to frantic questions, often demands from reporters and airline and hotel employees, and then telling them that everything was going to be all right.

Bob Manning was the master. He was an attractive man with graying hair who looked like a corporate vice president soon to be a corporate president. With a deep voice and a slightly Southern accent

Bob Manning in tan raincoat in Britain. Photo: Dennis Brack.

he would assure people that everything was under control or would be in the very near future. Hugh Sidey of *Time* wrote of Manning: "He was calm and shrewd and as smooth as sour mash from Tennessee, from which he hailed. He never failed." Those who knew Manning realized that there was a great deal going on behind his calm demeanor and that their problems really would be solved. They called him "the Silver Fox."

The transition from trains to planes had increased the amount of travel expense for the photographers, and there still were no free rides for the press. The travel office paid all of the expenses for the press—the plane charter, pool rental cars, pool telephone lines, the rental of the press rooms (usually a hotel ballroom which is a major expense), and so on. At the end of the trip the travel office divided the expense amount by the number of press on the trip and billed the news organizations on the trip. When a large number of reporters and photographers traveled, the rule of thumb for trip costs would be the highest first-class fare plus fifty percent. (Today, the number of traveling press has decreased so there are fewer organizations to share the expenses.) Each press person on a presidential trip paid for his or her hotel rooms and meals. The hotel room charges were not part of the expenses calculated by the travel office. The press pool riding on Air Force One, instead of the plane charter, paid the same amount as those on the press charter. That money was paid back to the White House.

If you could afford the fare and had the ability to obtain the proper press accreditation, the press charters were a pretty good deal. The cost was high, but on what other tour might you pal around with CBS's Walter Cronkite or Dan Rather or NBC's John Chancellor, among others? Without a deadline to meet, a newspaper owner or publisher could attend the open press events and witness a bit of history.

The Johnson years were especially difficult for the travel office, not that the president cared. The staff had no idea about his weekend plans or were too scared of their boss to ask. When they did ask, Johnson would say one thing and later change his mind. Travel office chief Bob Manning would get a haircut at Milton Pitts' barber shop even when he did not need one. Pitts would come to the White House to cut Johnson's hair, so Manning would go to Pitts' shop and discreetly ask if the president had mentioned anything about his weekend plans while getting a trim.

On one trip aboard Air Force One the press pool got a little extra for their travel dollar. The plane suddenly dropped three thousand feet, scaring the devil out of everyone. Sometime later, Johnson came back to the press area. "You know," the president said, "if this plane had of gone down, you all would have gotten your names in the paper. Of course, it would have been in the small print."

Yoichi Okamoto was the first official presidential photographer and perhaps the best presidential photographer. Okamoto—everyone called him Oke—got his job easily, but keeping it was another matter. He began his government service in the Signal Corps and worked his way up to become director of visual services for the United States Information Agency. He accompanied Vice President Johnson on a trip to Berlin and Johnson loved the photographs that he made. Shortly after Johnson took office he did not like the photographs that were being made of him by the military photographers. He remembered Okamoto's photographs and issued an order: "Get me that Jap photographer."

White House photographer Yoichi Okamoto.
Photo: Lyndon B. Johnson Presidential Library.

An ability to make his pictures in an unobtrusive manner, coupled with a journalist's eye, were half of what made Okamoto the best of what would become a long line of presidential photographers. The other half was Okamoto's will to stand up to Johnson and demand that he be allowed the access that he needed to make his photographs. Everyone who knew Okamoto was an admirer of him as a man and a professional.

"Oke had class," remembered John Durniak, former picture editor of *Time*. "When he talked to people, they felt they were in the hands of a responsible individual, somebody who would not take advantage of them. I think that was one of the things that appealed to President Johnson. Oke was a student of human behavior. He understood President Johnson's moods. He knew where he should shoot and when it would be intrusive. He also knew that if Johnson read him out, it might be for five minutes, or five days, or five weeks. But it wasn't forever. They had one hell of a relationship, the depth of which only Oke knew."

Ironically, it was Jack Kightlinger, a Signal Corps photographer on Okamoto's staff, who made one of the most telling photographs of the Johnson White House years: the president tearful and alone in the Cabinet

President Johnson listening to an audio tape account of losing men in combat in Vietnam. Photo: Jack Kightlinger, the White House.

Room as he listened to an audiotape account of losing men in battle in Vietnam.

The assassinations of Martin Luther King Jr. and Robert Kennedy, the Vietnam War and the protests, and Johnson's own attitude and management style made for a somber and combative White House in Johnson's last months in office. The president was always playing people off against each other. The press and Secret Service were his favorites. During a trip to Austin, Johnson was walking through a hotel lobby and some members of the press were right with him shouting questions that he did not want to answer. The president snarled at his Secret Service agents, "You can't keep these reporters away from me, and you're supposed to be my protection?"

Do You Like Your Job?

Richard M. Nixon

The morning after President Richard M. Nixon's second inauguration, in January 1973, many newspapers carried on their front pages a large photograph of Nixon taking the oath of office. Over the president's shoulder, standing out in a sea of black formal morning coats, was photographer Cecil Stoughton, wearing a bright, red-checkered hunting coat and taking pictures. At the time, Stoughton was the chief photographer for the National Park Service, and he had received a general pass to cover the event.

A story went around the news photographers at the White House that the president himself pointed to Stoughton in the photograph and asked an aide who the photographer worked for. You, the aide said. Not anymore, Nixon was said to have replied. While that might be apocryphal, what happened to Stoughton was well-documented. His job at the Park Service was abolished within days of the inauguration after White House officials expressed annoyance that he was in many of the photographs taken as Chief Justice Warren Burger administered the oath of office. Stoughton told the *New York Times*, "They should have told me they didn't want me on the stand."

President Nixon taking the oath of office. Behind him is photographer Cecil Stoughton in a red-and-white checkered hunting jacket. Photo: Dennis Brack.

That story aside, in many ways Nixon and the news photographers covering the White House got along very well, at least during the first part of his administration. The creative advance work of Ron Walker during the campaign along with the photo wrangler, Tim Elbourne, created useable pictures for the photographers covering Nixon. If the pictures were good, the photographers were happy. There was a feeling that the photographers were dealing with competent pros who knew the business. Sure, they were working for their man and everyone knew it. The good friendships and respect that developed continued, even during the difficult Watergate days.

One group did not care for the photographers who covered Nixon's presidential campaign: Cadillac dealers. Greeting the photographers at every campaign stop were two shiny, new Cadillac convertibles, tops down. The photographers piled into the back seats and looked behind them at the candidate's car. Along the curbs, the crowds would start to build, Nixon would stand up in his car to wave, and the photographers would ease up to the top of the backseat to make their pictures. There would be a muffled *thump!* and the driver would ask about it—if he could hear the sound over the noise of the

Candidate Nixon campaigning in Pennsylvania in 1968. The photographers' car was usually in the right position to make good photographs. Photo: Dennis Brack.

crowds. The photographers knew but no one would say. When the press plane took off, the driver would raise the Cadillac's top and find the source of the thumping sound: the glass window of the convertible top had cracked. It happened every time.

The Nixon presidency's most lasting mark on the White House press corps was a change in their work space: the press room. That an

Reporters running from the Fishroom through the old White House lobby to the pressroom to file the report of the end of World War II. Photo: WHNPA archive.

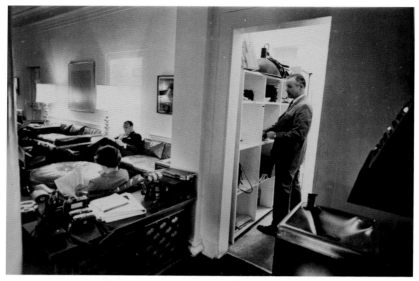

Bruce Hoertel works with his equipment off the press lobby. Photo: WHNPA archives.

area in the White House would be provided to the press dates back to President Theodore Roosevelt. He had noticed a group of reporters standing outside the Northwest Gate of the White House at the end of the driveway that leads to the West Wing. In accordance with the custom of the time, they were waiting to interview presidential visitors as they came through the gate. The journalists would ask the visitors what they had discussed with the chief executive, in the hope of picking up some news. The weather on this particular day was inclement. The reporters were cold and wet. Roosevelt decreed, "Let us set aside a room for them in the West Wing." And so it was done.

The West Lobby door of the White House led to the press area. You would open that door and walk a few feet into a large, dark room that would make you want to take a nap. The sinking spell was triggered by dim light and the large leather couches around the room. They were supposed to be reserved for official visitors, but the large men who were stretched out on them in various states of intense relaxation discouraged any visitor from asking for a place to sit. The room was rather worn and very messy. It was probably very dirty, too, but you could not tell because it was so dark. A large, wide Philippine

The White House press work area before the major remodeling during the Nixon administration. Photo: WHNPA archives.

mahogany table was under a chandelier in the middle of the room. The table was originally used for visitors to leave their coats and hats, but that was impossible because this was where "the stills" put their gear, reporters put their typewriters, and just about everything else went if it was not left on the floor.

The White House police reception desk was to the left at the entrance of the lobby. A hall to the left of the reception desk led to the press office staff and the office of the press secretary. The next door on the left led to a room often used for press briefings. The reporters' work area was a small room to the right of the lobby door. A baffle at the entryway blocked people from looking into the work area and on it was a framed copy of a bill signed by President Lyndon Johnson and a selection of his signing pens. A table with phones, typewriters, and paper—lots of paper—ran down one side. There were small desks along the south wall and that was it with the exception of two 1940's wooden phone booths. The corner desk of Bob Nixon of the International News Service was the most popular area in the room because it doubled as a table for games of "Puke," a seven-card stud

The new press briefing room during the Nixon years.

game popular with the press corps. "Everyone played," recalled Henry Burroughs, "reporters, photographers, soundmen, and an occasional guard. One member of the White House staff used to join the game almost daily."

The room often used for press briefings, located across a small hall next to the Oval Office, became known as the "Fishroom" because President Franklin D. Roosevelt kept some fishing trophies and his aquariums there. (Today, it is named the Roosevelt Room.) Often the reporters were called into the Fishroom for important announcements. Large groups visiting the president had their meeting there, which meant that they had to come and go through the press lobby and be available to the reporters for interviews. Such awkward situations for official visitors, plus the growing numbers of the press covering the White House, prompted a renovation.

Most observers thought the main reason for the change was the desire by Henry Kissinger, then the president's national security adviser, to have a larger office. Nixon left for an extended vacation to the Western White House and the carpenters went to work. When he

The White House press briefing room today. Photo: Dennis Brack.

returned, Kissinger had a new office that was about the size and in the exact space of the old press work area. The contractors had carefully put boards around the tiles of Franklin Roosevelt's swimming pool. Since children had sent their dimes to help pay for the pool it is an important part of American history. The pool is still there, but

The photographers' work area today. Mike Reynolds, European Press Association, Larry Downing, Reuters, and Mandel Ngan, AFP, check their equipment. Photo: Dennis Brack.

it is covered by a floor. On top of this floor is the new White House press briefing room. It did not have the theater chairs that it has today. The plush, glamorous style, more sixties Las Vegas casual than White House business, prompted Pete Lisagor of the *Chicago Daily News* to remark, "Well, I'll have a drink, but I won't go upstairs.'"

The press work area was located behind the briefing room in a space that had been the laundry room for the dirty clothes of President Theodore Roosevelt. I guess it is fitting that the space is used to deal with the dirty laundry of presidents today.

Major events of the Nixon presidency often involved international travel. *Time* correspondent Hugh Sidey observed, "For a Washington reporter or photographer the only thing worse than being on a presidential trip is not being on the trip." At least the food was good on press charters—first-class and safe to eat anywhere in the world. What was served at the presidential palaces the press visited might have been wonderful for the local invited guests, but not for working photographers. Many a smart photographer covering presidential trips would follow the ways of Cleve Ryan, the White House pool electrician. He would bring along a bag with cans of tuna fish. No local food would be eaten by Ryan, but he found that the beer was good everywhere.

There was one time when the photographers broke their own

The forty-five minute ride into New Delhi on a fast flatbed truck. Photo: Dennis Brack.

rules about the foreign cuisine. The first day of a presidential visit to India in 1969 was a bear. It was hot, extremely hot. The airport was forty-five miles from New Delhi. After an airport greeting ceremony, the photographers were loaded into a farmer's truck. Outside the airport, Nixon and the president of India rode in open cars and waved to the crowds, then the motorcade halted briefly and the presidents transferred to limousines. The photographers remained in the farmer's truck. For the next forty-three miles the motorcade headed to New Delhi at speeds that put the farmer's truck to the test. The photographers suffered the hot wind in their faces and tried to keep low. The Indian advance team had done a practice run with the farmer's truck, but it was without people standing in the back. Several low bridges that the motorcade passed under would have decapitated anyone standing.

Finally, the motorcade stopped, the presidents returned to their open car, and the real parade began. Millions of Indians cheered. The motorcade must have gone down every major street of New Delhi. The ride, the heat, and the crowds lasted for at least an hour until the presidents stopped in front of the Indian Presidential Palace. There was another arrival ceremony to be photographed. The presidents and their wives went into the palace and the photographers remained in the sun. An advanceman took pity and the photographers were allowed to step inside.

Two Indian servants carrying a tray of cups and a bowl of water entered the holding room. The water looked a bit murky and the cups were not all that clean, but this was India, after all. The American photographers grabbed the cups and dipped them in the water for a much-needed drink. The Indian photographers began to make pictures of the event. It was not until the next day when they saw the pictures in the local newspaper and had the headline translated that the Americans realized their mistake. The headline read: "United States photographers drink water used to rinse the ice cream cups from the first ladies tea."

The Nixon visit to China in 1972 was historic in improving relations with the world's most populous nation. No American president

Dirck Halstead and John Dominis wait for President Nixon's arrival in Beijing. Dirck Halstead Collection, Briscoe Center for American History.

had been to Beijing. Yet the Chinese limited the number in the presidential party, and that meant the number of press was cut to a minimum. The news organizations sent their best photographers: Horst

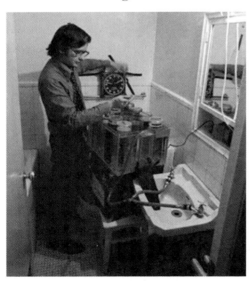

Dirck Halstead in his color darkroom, a Beijing hotel bathroom. Dirck Halsted Collection, Briscoe Center for American History.

Faas and Bob Daugherty for the Associated Press, Frank Cancellare and Dirck Halstead for United Press International, Wally McNamee for *Newsweek*, and John Dominis for Time Inc. These "stars," accustomed to the support of others, had to remember old skills, which included developing their own film.

Most of the press on the trip were thankful to be selected and worked like crazy, but one network anchor remained a prima donna and gave the camera crews a bit of a hard time. On the final day of the tour it was payback time. The Chinese thought everything the Americans had was extremely valuable. Helpful Chinese were constantly running after the Americans to return their discarded rubbish. It was impossible to throw anything away. The television crews were still shooting 16mm film so there was a world of waste—film boxes, roll ends, and so on. After the prima donna had checked out of her room, the crews brought all of their trash into her room. Sure enough, as the press bus was ready to roll towards the airport, a phalanx of Chinese carrying large bags came scurrying out to return her treasures. Everyone enjoyed watching her deal with it.

Nixon flew to the Middle East in June 1974 as part of an effort to improve American relations with the region. Egyptian President Anwar Sadat greeted Nixon in Cairo, and the two leaders waved from an open car as they traveled through the city, cheered along their route by more than one million people. On the first night of the trip, Sadat hosted a dinner for the American president. While the two leaders sat in the front row for the evening's entertainment, the five pool photographers stood in the back. They were just watching because they thought they had made the pictures for the day—the greeting, the motorcade, the crowds. Suddenly, a belly dancer began performing not two feet from Nixon and Sadat. The photographers rushed down the aisle to make pictures. The photographs of the belly dancer arching to a full "U" in front of Secretary of State Henry Kissinger made the front pages of papers throughout the world.

Everyone there remembered the warm night, the festive tents, and the buffet of food that went to infinity. The next morning the photographers remembered the food with a feeling of nausea and deep regret. Dennis Cook, working for United Press International, was down and out so the other photographers took one of his cameras on a tour of the pyramids with the first ladies. Mrs. Nixon probably had a remembrance of the previous night's dinner because everyone was moving very slowly that frightfully bright day. The photographers would make a picture and then one would ask, "Where's Dennis's camera?" and then they would make one for Cook.

Networks had used 16mm film since the beginning of television coverage of the White House. For President Nixon's trip to the Middle East in June 1974, CBS turned to videotape and sent their best team: cameraman Bob Dunn and soundman Arnie Jenson out of the Los Angeles bureau. Dunn and Jenson were very large men who knew their trade. Dunn had started in the movie business and actually worked with Ronald Reagan on various movies.

While in Saudi Arabia the first lady went shopping in Jeddah at the Gold Souq, an open-air marketplace specializing in jewelry. The CBS video crew went along with about two hundred pounds of equipment. Connie Chung was the CBS correspondent on the story. Chung wore a short skirt cut above the knee, which was the most revealing outfit that the hundreds of Saudi men cramming into the souq had ever seen. She looked to be clearly in charge of Dunn and Jenson, and that was more than the minds of the Saudi men could compute.

Dunn carried the gigantic camera while Jenson handled an equally large recording device. A third man pushed a flatbed cart of brand-new car batteries that powered this new system. All of these machines were connected by a giant cable. It snaked through the massive crowd and tripped

Correspondent Connie Chung covering first lady Pat Nixon's visit to the Gold Souq in Jeddah, Saudi Arabia. Photo: Dennis Brack.

up everyone as they followed Mrs. Nixon. When the car battery charge was used up, they would leave the battery in the street, sparking a small riot among the Saudis who wanted that prize. At one point the entire

President Nixon looks through the viewfinder of camera-man Bob Peterson's Arriflex during a photo op at the WHNPA contest winners. Photo: WHNPA.

entourage crossed a street and Chung actually stopped traffic.

Nixon really did not care about photographs. His idea of a good photo came from his days as a congressman and senator from California. Get three people on one side, three people on the other side, and Nixon in the middle—then take the picture. He had gotten to know photographers like Frank Cancellare and Henry Griffin while on Capitol Hill. He did come to the White House News Photographers Association dinners, but he had no favorites. He kept photographers at arm's length. No friends but no enemies, no disrespect—and sometimes he kind of showed he cared.

On a trip to Europe with Nixon, I stumbled and fell while Nixon was working a crowd in Berlin, but I was not hurt. The next day, in Rome, I was walking backward and making pictures—we called that "back peddling"—in front of Nixon after he was finished laying a wreath at the Victor Emmanuel Monument. The president looked over and said: "Now be careful. We don't want you taking a fall like yesterday."

There could be awkward moments with Nixon. One took place during a routine presidential motorcade. One of the police motorcycles escorting the line of vehicles skidded and crashed. The mo-

The Nixons pose on the first of three photo ops at the new Western White House. Photo: Dennis Brack.

torcade stopped, Nixon got out and made his way over to the injured patrolman, who had been pinned under his motorcycle. Nixon leaned over and asked, "Do you like your job?"

The Western White House, located in San Clemente, California, underwent a renovation and the president and first lady Pat Nixon wanted to show it to the traveling press. Their idea was to pick three locations for the writers and photographers to view and then the press would leave their cameras, tape recorders, and pencils at the front door and join them for a cocktail at their pool. Press secretary Ron Ziegler asked photographer Charlie Tasnadi and me to go to the Nixon home on the morning of the press viewing and reception and pick the best three locations.

That evening the traveling press arrived, photographed the Nixons at the three "photo opportunity" locations that we had selected, put down their equipment, and went on the house tour. Since Tasnadi and I had seen the home while selecting the locations, we went directly to the pool. The Nixons were alone and waiting for their guests. Tasnadi began to visit with Nixon and I went over to talk to the first lady. I tried every subject that I could think of and received that polite, turn-off expression that showed she had had the conversation hundreds of times. That is, until I said "tacos." The first lady lit up. She started telling me about the best places to eat tacos down the Pacific Highway, tacos sauces that she liked. She was excited and happy. You never know.

Even at the height of Watergate, Nixon showed a bit of concern for the photographers. Then again, it might have been a sense of humor seldom seen. On a live television address to the nation, the photographers had always gone into the Oval Office to make a few pictures after the president has made his speech. On the night that Nixon announced that he would release transcripts of the tape recordings made in the Oval Office, a large bookshelf holding the transcripts was to the left of the president.

John Full, a United Press International photographer, had been sleeping on one of the couches in the press room and had not paid any attention to the television address. Full joined the queue of photographers and went into the Oval Office. Every photographer went to the left so they could get the president in the foreground with the transcripts in the background. Not John Full. To avoid battling the crush, he went way over to the right. But that meant he would not be able to get the president and the transcripts in the same picture. Nixon looked over at Full, pointed to where the other photographers were shooting away, and said, "Young man, I think that you might want to be over there." Full noticed the transcripts for the first time and hurried to make a frame before they called "lights."

While the Watergate story brought Pulitzer Prizes to some reporters, it brought a gift to the still and video photographers and technicians—overtime. The story was a gift that kept on giving. Crews sat in front of houses all over Washington. Men and women sat on their campstools and may have grumbled about the weather, but the smiles returned when they calculated their overtime. These stakeouts were not just random events, they were everywhere, every day, and some were for the full 24 hours of the day. The stakeout at presidential aide John Dean's house in Alexandria, Virginia (we never caught him there) lasted for more than six months. Many video journalists built large additions to their homes that they named "The Watergate Wing."

On August 8, 1974, Nixon addressed the nation to announce that he was going to resign the presidency at noon the next day. The speech was live from the Oval Office and CBS was the network pool. The Nixon staff ordered that the cables were to be run from the Oval Office to the CBS truck and there were to be only two people in or around the Oval Office at the time of the speech.

Live remotes were technical challenges in those days and they had to be done with studio cameras. The producers gave two orders to the crew: No one was to have direct eye contact with the president, and no one was to speak to the president. George Christian was a studio technician. It was his first time in the Oval Office and he was nervous. Christian was to be there to fix the studio camera in case it broke during the live transmission. His only tool was a "greenie," a four-inch screwdriver with a green handle that could be used to adjust the tiny screws on the camera.

Minutes before the broadcast time, Nixon walked into the Oval Office alone. He sat at the desk, looked around the room and said, "Now would be a good time for anyone who doesn't need to be in this room to leave." There were only three people in the room: Christian, the cameraman, and a Secret Service agent. Christian was sure that the president was speaking to him, but he clutched his "greenie" and slid around the back of the camera to be as small as possible. This was difficult for Christian because he was a big man. The president skipped over the camera area and focused on the Secret Service agent. "Why are you still here?" Nixon asked. The agent replied, "I'm here to protect you." The president pointed to the door. Christian thought the agent retreated to the door, but he was too busy hiding to look.

Nixon addressed the nation and there were no technical glitches, but the night was far from over. The orders stood. There was to be no movement by the technical crew. They were prohibited from moving the equipment out or even leaving the Oval Office area—Nixon's orders. Christian spent the night sleeping on one of the equipment hampers (they were identical to those laundry hampers in hotels) along the colonnade outside the Oval Office. It was a warm August evening so he and the cameraman were comfortable. The president did not come into that area as he was known to do during his famous strolls around the White House grounds. Over the years, Christian went from technician to cameraman. He could be seen frequently on television as the cameraman who walked backward down the aisle with the president as he shook hands before and after the State of the Union address.

President Nixon's final double whammy. Photo: Dennis Brack.

Richard Nixon's final day as president was a time for classic photographs. The president had a reception in the East Room to say goodbye to his staff and then walked to the South Lawn and boarded Marine One. Photographers could do one event or the other but not both. As Nixon and the first lady walked toward the helicopter, six photographers stood on stepladders to see over the honor guard, perfect positions. The Nixons' walk down the red carpet and entry into Marine One had to be made with one camera. There was no time to change cameras or lenses. The photographers timed their shots; they only had thirty-six exposures on a roll of film.

Everything was fine until Nixon walked up the ramp to the helicopter and turned to face the crowd on the lawn. First, there was a wave, almost a salute—better get that, it might be all there is. Then he continued with his right arm, bringing it across his face and holding his hand high above—certainly want that. The photographers' prayers started: "Lord, please let me be on frame thirty-one and not frame thirty-five." Finally, the classic Nixon Double Whammy, his arms straight out and both hands making the "V" sign. The Nikon motor drives were zinging away. Some photographers got the picture and were happy, some did not and were not so happy. But all wanted Nixon to just get in the helicopter so that they could rewind and reload.

Not a Typical President

Gerald R. Ford

During the final days of the Nixon administration, photographers assigned to cover the White House were trying to get any image of the president. Nixon walking to and from the Old Executive Office Building was their best chance. Some said the doors to the press briefing room were locked during these crossings so the press could not run outside and take a look.

Photographers inside the press room did not care; other crews from their publications were at the East and West gates of West Executive with 600mm lenses. The outside photographers waited from morning until it was too dark to make a useable picture. The long lenses just fit between the bars of the gates, but the photographers had to move quickly when the gates were opened for government vehicles.

Across the Potomac River, off of Janneys Lane in Alexandria, Virginia, another group of still photographers and network crews relaxed in their camp chairs and enjoyed the hospitality of Vice President Gerald Ford's neighbors. Lasting friendships were made with these gracious people. Long after the Fords had moved into

The Fords pose for a picture in front of their home off Janneys Lane in Alexandria, Va. Photo: Dennis Brack.

the White House, some crews dropped by just to visit with the friends they had made during the Ford stakeout.

From time to time the vice president's wife, Betty Ford, or their daughter Susan would appear while leaving the house or coming home; they would yell a greeting. If photographers needed a special picture, the Fords invited them inside and they were welcome to stay and talk for a bit after the pictures were made.

Ford had been a congressman from Michigan since 1949 and was minority leader when Nixon chose him to replace Spiro T. Agnew as vice president in 1973. Photographers like George Tames, Jim Atherton, and Arthur Scott had been Jerry Ford's friends for years. He was comfortable with who he was and therefore at ease when photographers were around. Many new friends like Frank Johnston and Fred Ward had been made during the brief time he was the vice president.

"He had a style, he had an honesty, he had a demeanor that is not typical of presidents," Ward remembered. "Normally they are difficult to be around at close range—they don't like it, they're apprehensive. And he had none of those characteristics."

There is no doubt that the warm relationship between the Fords and the photographers was because of David Hume Kennerly, a *Time* photographer who became the official White House photographer when Ford replaced Nixon. The president would walk with photographers and before long would ask, "Have you been keeping Kennerly in line?" When a photographer had a good idea for a picture or a project, Kennerly would try to make it happen.

Sometimes the requests were rather strange. Dick Swanson had the idea of photographing Ford from the bottom of the White House swimming pool, looking up at the president as he made his morning swim. Any press office bureaucrat would have said that was absurd and turned down the request. Kennerly thought it would make a good picture. Early one morning Swanson was at the bottom of the White House pool with his waterproof Nikons. The photograph ran large in *People* magazine and won a prize in the White House News Photographers Association "Eyes of History" photographic contest.

Actually, all of the photographers wanted to photograph the president using the White House swimming pool. Ford's solution: Invite them all. On a weekend morning, the president came down to the pool wearing a white terrycloth robe. There was no presidential seal on the robe; this president did not need the presidential power symbols. The robe off, the president made a respectable dive and swam a couple of laps—Leicas clicked away, motor drives whirled. When the laps were over he came out of the pool and just stood and talked. He probably heard a couple of jokes from photographers that morning. It was hard to imagine any other president in that situation.

The photographers and President Ford in the White House pool. Photo: David Hume Kennerly.

President Ford laughs at a photographer's joke after an early morning swim in the White House pool. Photo: Dennis Brack.

Kennerly contributed more to the Ford presidency than his photographs. He might not admit it, but he worked at getting the president and his staff to "lighten up" just a little in those turbulent times. While he had the skills of Yoichi Okamoto of not being a distraction, he used his sense of humor (and his brain) at the right times to bring just a little joy to some very serious people. For example, Kennerly thought that the pictures made by the official White House photographer should not be used by the presidential campaign. The Ford re-election committee hired me to make the photographs for Ford campaign posters and brochures.

One day as I was following Kennerly and making pictures of the president at work, Ford finished up a meeting and was about to move to the next room. Kennerly whispered a suggestion to me: We would stand on each side of the door and "stand post" like Secret Service agents. We went to each side of the door, stood straight with our hands clasped in our best Secret Service pose, and looked ahead. Ford walked up, looked at us, then smiled and shook his head as he went through the door. For this particular president, it was the right thing to do.

The photographers lightened up, too, at times with practical jokes. One of the best was played on Eddie Adams during Ford's trip to China in 1975. As with the Nixon visit, the Chinese limited the number of Americans and that applied to the number of photographers. Adams was on the trip for *Time* and shooting negative color in part to make a photo of Chinese leader Deng Xiaoping that would make a *Time* cover. Everyone was working long hours and not eating. Adams rushed into the hotel room that had its bathroom set up as a darkroom, raving about his great pictures. He was sure he had a cover shot on one of his two rolls of color negative film. He set his film down on a dresser and left to find something to eat. Then evil minds went to work.

They took his two rolls of film and set two identical but unexposed rolls in the exact place that Adams had left his rolls. When he returned, Adams picked up the fake rolls and went into the bathroom turned darkroom. At the time when it was thought that he would have his film out of the containers and ready for spooling onto the developing tank reels, a photographer banged on the door and announced that he really needed to use the bathroom. Adams shouted, "Developing—don't come in!" The intruder opened the door wide and Adams shouted while trying to shield the film between his legs. He was certain that his great photographs had been ruined, and he was angry. It took a while for him to calm down even after the photographers produced his rolls of film.

The best day of the Ford years, at least for photographers, was July 4, 1976, the nation's bicentennial. To celebrate the two hundredth birthday of America, Ford began the day across from the White House with a service at St. John's Episcopal Church, Lafayette Park. He went on to birthday events at Valley Forge in Pennsylvania, the Liberty Bell in Philadelphia, and the tall ships that had sailed into New York Harbor in the shadow of the Statue of Liberty. Aboard the USS *Nashville*, Ford reviewed the ships. The press pool was with Ford all the way for wonderful pictures.

That evening, one more picture was needed to complete the day of celebration: the president and first lady, back in Washington, watching what was billed as the nation's largest fireworks show on the National Mall. The Fords were going to watch from the Truman Balcony of the White House. Minutes before the show began, an advanceman escorted to the balcony four photographers—Charles Bennett of the Associated Press, Dirck Halstead of *Time*, John Full of

Charles Bennett, Associated Press; Dennis Brack, Black Star; Dirck Halstead, Time; John Full, United Press International, and President Ford on the Truman balcony of the White House, July 4, 1976. Photo: David Hume Kennerly, the White House.

United Press International, and me, then with Black Star. Fireworks photographs require a long exposure—about six seconds—and all of us had our cameras mounted on tripods. We agreed to use one strobe on a stand to light the Fords. We returned to the methods of the photographers using flash powder: The photographer triggering the strobe light would say, "Open shutter." When everyone had their shutters open recording the fireworks burst, the strobe would be triggered to illuminate the president and first lady.

The Fords were in position and the fireworks show began, but the fireworks were exploding over to the right side. It was going to be a long show and they were going to work their way into the place that the photographers wanted for their picture. The advanceman told us he was sorry that the arrangements did not work out and started to usher us off the balcony. And we started groaning. Once again, Ford had a better idea. "Get these fellows a drink," he told an aide. To us, he said, "You can have your party over here and we'll be over there. Just call us when the fireworks are where you want them."

After a very long day, the gin and tonics tasted so good. Two drinks and some delicious appetizers later, the fireworks were just right for the photo and we asked the Fords to join us. I was control-

The Fords pose for a photo when the fireworks were in the right place for a photograph. Photo: Dennis Brack.

ling the one strobe and, I must admit, on the first round I triggered the strobe and then quickly said, "Open shutter." Another round of groans from the photographers. Our timing improved and we got the pictures we wanted. It was a great way to celebrate the Bicentennial.

What kind of a president was this person? Ford got a reputation for being clumsy after a few missteps and mishaps. The photographs of him bumping his head on the door of Marine One and falling down the steps of Air Force One in Salzburg, Austria, were a major reason his press secretary, Larry Speakes, complained that "the press was determined to make him look like a klutz." The idea that Ford was physically awkward would hurt his re-election campaign when he ran against Democrat Jimmy Carter in 1976. Ford could have considered the photographers his enemy, but he did not. He knew that they were only doing their jobs. Photographs of Ford taking a tumble while skiing got major play and Associated Press photographer Charles Tasnadi, an expert skier, made his share of them. That never stopped Ford from visiting with Tasnadi, and the president often asked him to share a chairlift on the ride up the ski slope.

President Ford searches for his ball at the Bob Hope Open in Palm Springs, California. Photo: Dennis Brack.

What kind of a person was this president? Photographer Fred Ward spent three months behind the scenes during the Ford years on a book, *Portrait of a President.* He used available light with 35mm black and white, but on one occasion he had a color assignment in the Oval Office. Color in the seventies meant strobes and the large Thomas Strobes required electricity. While Ward searched for a plug, he looked over and was surprised to see Ford on his hands and knees behind the couch. My God, Fred thought, the president has had a stroke, a heart attack, something horrible. Ford looked up and said, "I think Cleve plugs his light in somewhere around here." Cleve Ryan was the television networks' electrician. At that moment, this president was just a person trying to help a friend.

Very Frustrating Times

Jimmy Carter

He seemed to love humanity. People who evoke his compassion were certain to receive a caring embrace and perhaps one of his forehead-to-forehead moments. President Jimmy Carter's love for other individuals who were close to him, even those who might be called on to give their lives to protect him—not so much. It was as if those people were not worth his time and attention. He simply did not want to be bothered with them. Secret Service agents and the executive mansion staff were some of the little people in the Carter White House, instructed to never say hello and never to speak unless spoken to. He ignored them as he passed. The lowest on his list of little people were the photographers.

Carter did his duty of carrying on a tradition that began with Franklin D. Roosevelt of posing with the winners of the White House News Photographers Association contest, but that was it. For some reason he never acknowledged the existence of photographers and never called to the "regulars" by name as many other presidents had.

Carter's top staff had about as much interest in photographers as their boss. His press secretary, Jody Powell, once described the lower press office in the White House as "the first line of defense between the leader of the free world and the barbarians in the press room." The only thing about photography that they were sure of was that they did not want another David Hume Kennerly running around the White House as an official photographer. The existing staff of official photographers stayed, but they were not granted behind-the-scenes access.

On his first day in office the photographers were positioned at the presidential limousine to photograph a confident new president on his way to tell various government agencies about the new "Carter era" in Washington. He slipped. It was just a tiny patch of ice, but he hit it just right. His arms went up and his briefcase went flying. The photographs were on the front page of every newspaper the next day and the Carter honeymoon with the press was over. The feud began and kept growing.

One incident that illustrated their lack of interest and knowledge about still pictures involved the world-famous portrait pho-

tographer Yousuf Karsh. *Time* magazine was writing a cover story on Carter's men, Powell and chief of staff Hamilton Jordan. It was a favorable story for the Carter presidency. *Time* commissioned Karsh to travel from his home in Ottawa, Canada, to make the cover portrait. For two days Karsh sat in the White House press room and waited for Powell and Jordan to find the time to pose for their portrait. When someone went to Powell and explained that Karsh was the foremost portrait photogra-

President Carter slips on his first walk from the Oval Office. Photo: Dennis Brack.

pher of the day and it was a big mistake to treat him like they handled other photographers, Powell quickly arranged for the photo session.

There were two "photo opp" modes for Carter: the big smile and wave mode or the serious, pensive mode. Occasionally he got the looks mixed. For his visit to the Berlin Wall, two stands were constructed. One was for the president to look over the Berlin Wall into East Germany. The other stand was for the pho-

Carter chief of staff Hamilton Jordan and press secretary Jody Powell. Photo: Dennis Brack, not Yousuf Karsh.

tographers to make pictures of the president looking over the wall. Carter climbed up the stairs, smiled, and waved at the other stand. After a few waves he must have thought better and quickly turned to his serious, pensive mode and stared at the wall and East Germany.

President Carter in serious pensive mode in Poland. Photo: Dennis Brack.

President Carter in big smile, wave mode in California. Photo: Dennis Brack.

Sometimes brash young men and women who took a condescending attitude toward photographers were chosen as advance people. This would be all right as long as they knew what they were doing and the photographers got the pictures that they needed to cover the story. It was not long before the photographers covering Carter realized that they were following two people who thought they knew everything but actually were clueless. Pools were running into locked doors, missing pictures, or denied access for pictures that they could have made. It made for very frustrating times.

Most in the press office were good people trying to make the best out of a bad situation, but mistakes and bad luck just kept happening. The photographers knew that the people in the press office were not to be blamed. The mistakes were not their fault. Perhaps the mistakes occurred because of the smaller press office staff. Carter had ordered that the press office staff was to be reduced thirty percent from the Ford administration.

Summer arrived and energy conservation became a top Carter priority. The staff would adjust the thermostats and the press would swelter like the president and the rest of the White House occupants. Mysteriously, the thermostat in the press area would be lowered and cool air would once more flow. The Interior Department maintenance staff placed a plastic cover with a lock around the press room thermostat, but the press area continued to be the coolest place in the White House. What the staff did not know was that the network electricians would place a 1,000-watt Lowell light close to the plastic-encased thermostat. The heat from the light would cause the temperature around the device to increase and tell it to increase the amount of air conditioning for that area.

During the Carter administration a White House electrical engineer checks the thermostat in the press work area. Photo: Dennis Brack.

The presidential visit to Iran over New Year's Eve 1977 was a strange time. The traveling press could feel the tension of a regime that was clinging to power. To show that life was normal, the administration of the shah of Iran put on lavish entertainment for Carter and for the traveling press. While the shah honored Carter at a state dinner, his government entertained the traveling press with a reception and dinner. The press and the Pan Am flight crew drank champagne and ate tons of caviar. The climax of the evening was to be the dinner. The doors opened and the traveling press, led by the Pan Am flight attendants, walked into the dining room. There was an abrupt about face when everyone saw five boar's heads staring back at them on trays placed down a long dining room table. The best dishes of the Middle East were placed around the heads. Perhaps parts of the boar were, too, but everyone had lost their appetites. Fortunately, the champagne was still flowing and the caviar trays had been refilled so the party continued in the reception area.

A few lucky members of the White House press remembered a pool in France in 1978 as one of the best meals that they ever experienced. On a three-hour train ride from Bayeux to Paris the pool enjoyed the French cooking that Carter and French President Giscard d'Estaing feasted on during their working luncheon in the

French president's railroad car. Perhaps it was the selections of the best French wines that led the entire press pool to say "no thanks" when offered an opportunity to photograph the two leaders at lunch. The train arrived and the motorcade zoomed out of the St. Lazare station in Paris with NBC News correspondent John Chancellor joining Percy, the NBC cameraman, on the tailgate of the station wagon. A "Tallyhoo!" was heard as the presidential motorcade turned toward the Marigny guest house. It had been a great lunch.

Carter traveled to Japan in 1979 to attend an economic summit. Economic summits were major stories in the seventies and eighties. It was planned as a long trip covering Japan and Korea, but the stop that was of particular interest to the members of the press was a three-day rest stop in Hawaii on the return. In Korea, Carter feared that pictures of the president and first lady relaxing on a beach would not be received favorably while Americans were waiting in long gas lines so he decided to return to Washington. No three-day rest stop. The press was not happy and decided to party. Drinks flowed, and soon a couple with their earphones on started dancing in the aisles. Others followed and the entire plane turned into a disco—not your average airline flight.

Naomi Nover was not your average correspondent. Always in a blue dress, sometimes one with white polka dots, she made all of the foreign trips during the Carter years—and those during the Reagan and George H.W. Bush administrations. Her husband, Barney Nover, had been a correspondent for the *Washington Post* and the *Denver Post*. When he retired in 1971 he founded the Nover News Service with his wife. After her husband's death, Naomi Nover kept her press credentials. No one could ever find a client for the Nover News Service, but that did not stop her. She would sign up for every foreign presidential trip and was the first to send in a check for the White House travel office invoice.

Naomi—everyone knew her by her first name—had a grandmotherly, Mrs. Doubtfire-like appearance that disguised an aggressive force not to be taken lightly.

Naomi Nover in full swing. Photo: Dennis Brack.

Photographers tried to give Naomi a wide berth, but it was difficult. She carried a point-and-shoot camera and thought she was entitled to be in the photographers' areas. During a trip to Britain, Carter was working a rope line in Newcastle when he lifted a plump, ugly baby. For photographer Dick Swanson, on assignment for *People*, it was a perfect picture. He did a "Hail Mary" over Naomi to take the photo. She turned so that she was facing Swanson, smiled, and with all her strength kneed him in the groin.

More than once, members of the White House travel office staff had to run to escape Naomi's umbrella as she swung it toward their heads. Hotel staff also could suffer her wrath. Naomi complained about her bill at one hotel, but the clerk told her that records showed that she had cleared out the mini bar. She opened her huge blue purse and dumped a refrigerator full of little bottles on the hotel's counter.

Naomi was always trying to sneak into press pools. When President Ronald Reagan and the first lady were touring the Terracotta Warriors in Xian, China, she was determined to get in the floor pool position. A Chinese guard blocked her. Gary Schuster, a reporter for the *Detroit News*, pointed to Naomi and showed the guard a one-dollar bill with its presidential portrait—Naomi did look a lot like George Washington—and told the guard, "Very famous." The guard

Naomi Nover with her "point and shoot" camera. Photo: Dennis Brack.

bowed and allowed her to join the photographers.

Few practical jokes were more elaborate than the Granville Withers hoax that unfolded during Carter's trip to South America and Africa. *Time* magazine had assigned a young photographer named Kit Luce to the trip. Luce was a good name to have at Time Inc., the company founded by publisher Henry Luce. And Kit Luce was a member of the family. On any presidential trip, there would be a certain amount of testing of the new photographers by the old hands. Kit Luce was found to be eager and gullible.

In Brasilia, the young Luce got a call from Mr. Granville Withers, the *Time* bureau chief in Rio de Janeiro—a fictional character played over the phone, with a perfect British accent, by AP photographer Bob Daughtery. Granville Withers told Luce that he had heard great things about him and would like to buy him a drink in the hotel lobby bar. Luce raced downstairs, looking for but not finding Withers. The hook was set.

For days Luce got notes and calls from Mr. Withers, always the same handwriting and voice, and he always found that Mr. Withers had just left. The other photographers joined in, telling Luce that they had just seen Mr. Withers, a sophisticated British fellow with a large mustache. The White House travel office was on board, too. At one stop just before the buses were about to roll, Billy Dale of the travel office stuck his head into the photographers' bus and asked, "Is Kit Luce here? There's a fellow out here named Withers who wants to talk to you." Dale disappeared, Luce raced to the front of the bus, got off and searched everywhere. Right on cue the buses rolled up a few feet, Luce panicked and raced back to the bus and his cameras.

Luce was the *Time* photographer designated to hand-carry the color film back to New York from Brazil. The Pan Am press charter crew knew the Pan Am crew on the Rio to New York flight and gave the purser another handwritten note from Granville Withers. After the 707 was airborne, the purser delivered the note to Luce, who was seated in the economy section. It read: "Had to fly to New York, please join me in the First Class cabin, Granville." The Pan Am crew, in on the joke, told Kit that he was not allowed in the first-class section and could not disturb a passenger there. Early in the morning, Luce was awakened by a call from Mr. Withers saying that he was sorry for the mix-up on the plane and inviting Luce to join him for an early breakfast. Mr. Withers never showed up.

Good food and good pranks aside, the best times for photographers during the Carter years were in Plains, Georgia, in the fall of 1976 as his campaign appeared to be on a winning path. There was an energy that came from being with a winner. Most of the Washington photographers had walked the red clay roads of Alabama and Georgia during the civil rights marches. Once more it was fun to work along the side of the legends of civil rights photographers like Joe Holloway Jr. of the Associated Press and Laurens Pierce of CBS News.

In the evenings the Georgia heat cooled, the merciless mosquitoes relented just a bit, and everyone gathered at Faye's Bar-B-Que Villa in Americus, Georgia. Carter's hometown of Plains had no hotels or motels and the press stayed ten miles up Route 280 in Americus. Faye Wells and her husband, David, saw an opportunity and went for it. They set up a restaurant in a doublewide trailer. David, a lieutenant in the Georgia Highway Patrol during the day, grilled steaks and boiled fresh corn outside and Faye did the salad inside in the kitchen. You did not want to look inside the closets of the trailer; they were full of their children's cloths. Most of the reporters and network crews ate on picnic tables and enjoyed thick steaks. From time to time Miss Lillian, Carter's mother, would come up from Plains for an evening at Faye's.

Everyone loved Faye Wells. She had never been out of the state of Georgia. On a Carter day trip to New York, the press persuaded the Carter folks to let her come on the press charter. She was treated to lunch at the midtown Manhattan restaurant '21' and a ride on the subway.

Four years later, stories about gas lines, the boycott of the Moscow Olympics, and the long-running hostage crisis in Iran had embittered both the press covering Carter and the president's press staff. The Carter campaign plane in 1980 was no longer the place to be for a photographer.

Carter's lack of interest in still photographs continued to the very end of his presidency. Just before the inauguration of Ronald Reagan, the world learned that the American hostages held in Iran for more than a year were freed. Carter was supposed to travel to Wiesbaden, Germany, to greet them. The date kept slipping back until the night of the inauguration. For days a Pan Am 747 had been standing at Andrews Air Force Base as the press charter for Carter. Since the press pays for time on the ground as well as in the air, the waiting produced a frightfully expensive trip for those covering the story.

The trip could have produced iconic photographs of grateful hostages embracing their former president. But over the Atlantic Ocean the former president's press secretary, Jody Powell, told the photographers that there would be no pool accompanying Carter into the military hospital at Wiesbaden Air Force Base. The photographers were flying to Germany and back for no pictures and were not happy.

Sure enough, the photographers rushed from the press vans to Carter's limousine. He got out and walked into the darkness up the path to the military hospital. After two hours he appeared alone walking back to the limousine. Instead of making pictures, Wally McNamee of *Newsweek* and I, working for *Time,* just held our hands out over our head in disgust. Carter saw us and figured it out. He turned around and walked back to the top of the steps of the hospital with former hostage Bruce

Laingen. They waved, and at least we had an image of Carter. Not a great image, but an image.

A Couple of Regular Guys

Ronald Reagan and George H.W. Bush

The candidate sets the tone of a presidential campaign. On Ronald Reagan's plane, a happy, easygoing atmosphere spread from the candidate to the staff, to the press, and even to the Secret

Candidate Reagan waves before boarding the campaign charter plane in 1976. Photo: Dennis Brack.

Nancy Reagan looks at "Ronnie" in one of the many farewell scenes on the campaign trail. Photo: Dennis Brack.

Service. Years after Reagan's 1976 campaign agents would come up to me and say, "You were on the Reagan campaign. Oh, that was the best."

Reagan had been a movie star before he was elected governor of California, but he was pretty much an ordinary guy. Photographer Ron Edmonds worked for United Press International out of the Sacramento bureau and was assigned to the Reagan campaign. Often the Reagans would stay at their Pacific Palisades home during the downtime of the campaign. The press would hang out along a wall to the side of the gate. One afternoon the hedges were being trimmed, but Edmonds thought nothing of it. Then he heard a familiar voice asking how he was doing. Reagan, hedge clippers in hand, was above Edmonds working on his hedges. Edmonds made a nice picture of Reagan at work. Edmonds knew his competition, the Associated Press, was on the way and asked Reagan, "How about clipping the hedges a little further into your yard?" Reagan agreed, which gave Edmonds an exclusive picture for that day.

There were at the very least two photographs to be made on the Reagan campaign. The first would be of the candidate speaking and the second was his wife, Nancy, watching her husband. "The look," as we called it, was a mixture of concentration and love. The regulars believed it was genuine. You just could not do that so many times

President and first lady Nancy Reagan at an inaugural ball. Photo: Dennis Brack.

without revealing that it was an act. The photographers thought Mrs. Reagan was a lady who most likely did not want to do some of the things or be in some of the places a campaign required. She was a good sport and the regular photographers on the Reagan campaign really liked her.

Magazine cover photo sessions were easy for Reagan, but there was one that did not go so well. During the Florida primary campaign I asked Reagan how his session with the esteemed photographer Richard Avedon went the day before. Reagan replied, "Oh, that photographer, he wasn't very good. I doubt if he got any pictures." Avedon was shooting a series on the candidates for *Rolling Stone* and during the photo session would make the candidate stand and wait. Reagan was used to working with Hollywood photographers. He would hear the shutter click and move on to another look for the photographer. The long periods of Avedon's time-consuming silence did not appeal to Reagan and it showed.

Most of the regulars were in the tight pool on the night of Reagan's first inauguration. We waited at the door of the diplomatic entrance of the White House to take the first pictures of the evening when the president and first lady came out to get into their limousine. Mrs. Reagan wore a sequined white dress and looked absolutely stunning. Oohs and wows came from the photographers, some of us saying, "You look beautiful." The new first lady looked at us a little sheepishly and said, "Come on, boys, it's only me."

The crowds at the inaugural balls were the largest that Washington had ever seen. In the pool car we could hear the radio traffic between the advance staff, Secret Service, and support staff. One transmission said, "Due to the crowds, the first couple will not have room to dance at the Kennedy Center." In response, someone said, "There must be some way?" The reply: "No, no way." There was a long pause. "You don't understand. Rainbow (the Secret Service code name for Mrs. Reagan) wants to dance at the Kennedy Center." The president and the first lady danced at the Kennedy Center.

Photographer Ron Edmonds of UPI was well-liked and respected by his peers and had bested the AP a number of times during the campaign, leading the AP to hire him at the Washington bureau. On March 30, 1981, Edmonds was on his second day of covering the White House when Reagan made a speech at the Washington Hilton. After the speech, Edmonds was first around the presidential limousine to make pictures of Reagan as he prepared to head back to the White House. Then Edmonds heard gunfire.

"When the first shot rang out, I saw the president's eyes flinch," he remembered. "I pushed the shutter down on my camera, which shoots six frames a second. Even at that speed, the Secret Service agents reacted so quickly that Reagan is only visible in three frames." The pictures he made were published on the front pages of newspapers around the world and on the covers of every newsmagazine and won a Pulitzer Prize.

Like President Jimmy Carter, Reagan never knew any of the photographers' names, but that was all right. He never knew anyone's name. Bill Fitzpatrick had been a White House staff photographer since the Nixon administration. Sometimes when Reagan wanted a picture taken, he would say, "Bring me the tall fellow."

The stewards who served presidents in the West Wing were Navy and were mostly chief petty officers. Reagan solved the problem of remembering their names by calling all of them "Chief." Most of the stewards were Filipino and a few were named Eduardo. That was good enough for Reagan. When he did not call the stewards "Chief" he called them all "Eduardo." One day Reagan was being served his coffee and as usual said, "Thank you, Chief." The steward politely said, "Begging your pardon, Mr. President, but I am not yet a chief. I am just a petty officer." Reagan decided to fix that. He picked up the phone, talked to someone, and then told the steward, "Now you're a chief." It was sort of a battlefield promotion.

Throughout her time as the first lady, Mrs. Reagan remembered the photographers who were on the early Reagan campaigns. *Time* magazine was doing a large story on a state dinner and one of the "must" photographs was a picture of the toasts. On all state dinners, the guests stood for the toasts, blocking the photographers in the back of the room. A solution was a remote camera mounted in a flower vase positioned behind the president. The only vase that would allow a hole for the camera was a six-sided wooden container. I cut a hole in each side and then sanded and painted the two vases white.

On the afternoon of the dinner, Mrs. Reagan came into the State Dining Room to check on the final arrangements. I had the two vases in position for her approval before the White House florist arranged the flowers, which were planned for the top of the vases. "Do we really have to do this?" she asked.

The White House florist and Nikon tech representative Ron Thompson talk about putting flowers in the top of the wooden flowers pots and remote cameras at the state dinner. Photo: Dennis Brack.

President Reagan giving a toast with the flower pot camera in the background. Photo: Dennis Brack.

The toast picture. Photo: Dennis Brack.

At that point Rex Scouten, the White House usher, said of course not. That could have been the end of the toast picture. As a last plea, I said that I had worked for six hours sanding and painting my flower pots. The first lady looked at the pots and then at me and said, "Okay, but don't put any flowers in the vases." The photograph worked and nobody noticed the containers—except for Howard Baker, the long-time senator from Tennessee and a chief of staff for Reagan. Baker himself was an excellent photographer.

Reagan was a great subject for the photographers. With his background in film and television he should have been, but there was more involved. Michael Deaver was an adviser to Reagan when he was governor and later when he was president, and Deaver was a very clever man. He had creative ideas for photos and knew the value of good advance work. Many of the best ideas came from Deaver, but others came from Steve Studdert and the advance team. They were smart, realizing that the people to ask about how to make the best photographs were the pros—the photographers who covered the White House. Perhaps the distance between the newsmakers and the news recorders came a bit close during that time, but everyone liked the idea of making things work smoothly and getting good photographs.

The Reagan advance teams were made up of people you could trust, people who wanted to do a great job. In addition everyone liked Michael Evans, the *Time* photographer whom Reagan had selected as the official White House photographer. Evans welcomed the participation of the newly formed "Turfbuilders," a group of the photographers from AP, UPI, *Time*, *Newsweek*, Black Star, and Sygma that helped to plan the still photographic coverage of papal visits, presidential trips, and other major events. There was no doubt that these photographers would be in the prime positions for covering the news.

The president's visit to Normandy on the fortieth anniversary of the D-Day landings was a great example of the Reagan White House at work. It illustrated the imagination involved in making things go perfectly and obtaining the photographs that his team wanted to see in newspapers and magazines. Presidents often visit Normandy Beach on June 6, the anniversary of the invasion of Europe during World War II. Reagan did not have a hard act to follow. Carter's wreath laying at the grave of Theodore Roosevelt Jr. in 1978 had been a disaster. The American pool had arrived ahead of the French pool and was standing in position. While Carter was on one knee doing his somber pose, the French pool plowed into the American photographers and the battle began. The Americans held their ground.

Five months before June 6, 1984, the Reagan staff began planning. In February they did "the survey," the first advance trip of a presidential visit. Senior representatives from the White House staff, Secret Service, and State Department considered the cities and sometime the countries to be visited and blocked out the major events of the trip. In late March the "pre-advance" went to France for the second stage of presidential visit planning. This larger group included representatives from the White House staff, Secret Service, State Department, Defense Department, and White House communications office. A representative from the television pool was always on

The Reagans walk to the grave of General Theodore Roosevelt Jr. in the U.S. Military Cemetery in Normandy, France. Photo: Dennis Brack.

the pre-advance, and a Turfbuilders representative was added—in this case, Larry Rubenstein from United Press International photos. The pre-advance spent some time at the cemetery because it was no secret that Deaver wanted a good, clean picture from that venue. Laying a wreath at the grave was one picture, but it had been done before many times. Someone thought that the best picture would be the Reagans walking through the field of crosses. How to get the president out of his limousine and to wander from point to point in a cemetery? An innovative advanceman had a solution: Give the Reagans two wreaths to lay. The first wreath to be laid would be many graves back and to the right of the photographers. The Reagans would then walk exactly through the area that would make the perfect photograph that everyone wanted.

On the advance trip, Rubenstein noted that the ground level view was not that exciting but the view from about five feet off the ground would give the field of crosses depth and symmetry. A riser was added to the "things to do list" of the advance team. One problem remained. The Secret Service agents were always close to the president, and men in dark suits would destroy the photograph. A deal was made that, for just the few seconds, the agents would move back to the edges of the borders of the photographers' frames. In the end, the picture worked perfectly and became one of the iconic photographs of the Reagan years.

A year later, the photographers had a different challenge at a different cemetery. Reagan had agreed to German Chancellor Helmut Kohl's request that the American president visit a German cemetery as a sign of reconciliation and good will. When a cemetery near the town of Bitburg was chosen, Reagan's advance team did not realize it contained the graves of a few dozen members of the Waffen-SS. The visit became embroiled in controversy over the idea that an American president would lay a wreath at a cemetery that contained the graves of Nazis. For the photographers the pressure was on to get Reagan and the SS graves in the same photograph.

Once that cold, dark morning was over and the pictures were made and shipped, the photographers had time to relax. The expanded pool met up with the rest of the White House press corps in a large hanger at a nearby NATO base. The traveling press had a long hold time while Reagan talked to some American troops, and there was a generous supply of Bitburg's famous beer. People were just milling around and talking as if it was a large cocktail party. A photographer—famous but nameless here—got a roll of toilet paper and lightly tucked the end under the belt in back of a White House advanceman who was making the rounds, asking how everything went. As the man walked around, the photographer gently rolled the paper out. Everyone but the advanceman saw what was going on and parted so the toilet paper tail would not be broken. The tables were around the side of the hanger so there was nothing to catch the toilet paper. People parted as the man walked throughout the hanger. People approached the advanceman and directed him with their conversation so that he would not double back. He never caught on. It could be a record for toilet paper tails.

The Reagans at Rancho del Cielo. Photo: Dennis Brack.

A voter's first look at a presidential candidate considers the person's ability to handle economic issues, foreign policy experience, family values, and so on. The members of the White House press corps have just one question: "Where does the candidate go on vacation?" Vacation coverage duty can be heaven or hell. Sometimes, not often, the president likes to vacation in miserable places. For example, Carter chose St. Simons Island, Georgia, and the press stayed at Jekyll Island. The mosquitoes and the smell of pulp paper plants made that a vacation to forget. Other presidents chose wonderful places but were so active that it was not a vacation for the press. I guess it should not be a vacation for the working press, but we could always hope.

Reagan passed the vacation test with flying colors. During his second term as governor, he and his wife purchased Rancho del Cielo, a small ranch in the Santa Ynez Mountains near Solvang, California. During his tenure in the White House, Reagan would go to the ranch every year and the press would have to spend his vacation time in nearby Santa Barbara. That helped to make presidential vacation duty at its absolute best. Once the Reagans went up the mountain, everyone knew that they were in and not to be heard from until the vacation was over.

The photographers usually hung out with advance or travel office staff who had two-way radios and would know if there were any breaking stories or pool calls. Some photographers did have to work during those ranch vacations. The nightly news shows needed footage as visuals to roll during the reporter's story on presidential issues. They found a clearing on one of the mountains that overlooked the ranch and named it Privacy Peak. Even with the 4,000mm mirror lens that CBS had rented, the quality was rough. Images of the Reagans' morning ride looked like glimpses of Bigfoot.

The crews took hours to get to the top of the mountain and they stayed up there for the entire day. It was all right for the men on the crews but not for camerawoman Ginny Vicario of ABC News, the only woman assigned to the coverage. One day the mountain crews heard the whoop of a large helicopter and looked up to see a portable toilet swinging in the wind. The helicopter hovered, the chain disconnected, and Vicario smiled. It was quickly named Ginny's Jon.

When Reagan met Soviet President Mikhail Gorbachev at the White House for the first time, in 1987, it was a major international news event. The White House and the Russians wanted it just that way. Every photographer was going to get a chance at the coverage, but the numbers were large even by White House counts. For the meeting picture the photographers were divided into waves, the American wires and magazines, Russians, international, and so on. There were about ten waves in all.

The American wires and magazines went first, but Reagan and Gorbachev were not seated and lights were called too soon. It was a disaster and the photographers told the advance staff. No problem, they said, just go around back and run through again as the last wave. Reagan and Gorbachev dutifully looked over at each other and shook hands for each wave. The last wave came into the room and Reagan looked over at the photographers. You could almost see his mind working: Wait a moment here. Haven't I seen these guys before—or am I starting to lose it? Whatever Reagan might have thought, he did not say a word.

Ask any Washington photographer who has been around for a while this question: "Who is the president that you have liked the most?" Chances are the answer will be George H.W. Bush, or Bush 41. He was a Washington animal, too, going back to his father's tenure in the Senate. Photographers were part of his childhood. Friendships were formed when Bush was a congressman from Texas and later when he was chairman of the Republican National Committee. During the race for president in 1980, those friendships were renewed and new ones made in the Iowa and New Hampshire primaries and on the presidential campaign when Bush was Reagan's running mate. In the Reagan years, Bush did what vice presidents do best: highlight issues that the president considers to be important. That meant more time with photographers and news crews.

Bush knew the photographers' names as anyone would know the names of their friends. He wanted to know something about each

On President George H.W. Bush's 65th birthday he is welcomed back to the White House by Richard Darman, the director of the Office of Management and Budget, in a gorilla costume. Darman couldn't see out of the suit and accidentally ran into his boss. Later, Darman told photographers that he thought that he might lose his job—no way with Bush. This president loved it. Photo: Dennis Brack.

photographer. As a young man I had put on a little weight—well, maybe a lot of weight. Once, after Bush had returned to Washington, he came over and congratulated me for taking off the pounds and asked me how I did it. Over the years as I was photographing him, Bush would say, "Still keeping the weight off—that's great." He did that kind of thing with all of his photographer friends.

His favorites were Scottie Applewhite, Dirck Halstead, and Larry Downing. Somewhere along the way Bush came up with a name for the group: "Photodogs." The photographers loved it, but one time it caused just a bit of bad press for the president. In 1989, on the first day of his trip to China, the presidential limousine stopped in the middle of Tiananmen Square. The crowds swarmed. The Chinese and American photographers raced up from the rear of the motorcade. Bush got out and stood on the rim of the limousine door. A tall man, he could be seen by the photographers shooting over the top of the limousine.

The picture everyone wanted was the president waving, the crowds behind him, and the portrait of Mao over the door of the Forbidden City. It was a difficult picture to make because of the

President Bush works with the "photodogs" to get the photograph they want in Tiananmen Square, China, on February 25, 1989. Photo: Susan Biddle, The White House.

crowds trying to shake hands with Bush. Joe Marquette of the Associated Press kept asking the president to wave this way, a little to the left, a little to the right, so that he could see the Mao portrait. Bush was doing his best to help with many smiles and waves, but finally he was finished and jokingly said to Marquette and the photo pool, "Oh, you photodogs have had enough." Then he climbed back into the limousine. The next morning the Beijing newspapers carried a headline, "The United States president calls his photographers dogs"—a grave insult.

After a long day of covering Bush's visit to Japan in 1992, a group of photographers had settled down for dinner at Wally McNamee's favorite restaurant in Tokyo, Shabu Shabu. Dirck Halstead, Mike Sargent, Charlie Archambault, Larry Downing, and Wally McNamee had winced at the extraordinarily high prices but ordered anyway. While they were enjoying their dinner the maitre d' came over to the table and said, "I'm so sorry for your president's sudden heart attack." With their adrenaline level as high as their bill, about $300 each, the photographers raced back to the press filing area.

Fortunately, there had been no heart attack, just an embarrassment for Bush. The television crews had been asked to leave the state dinner and return for the toasts. Without the knowledge of the White House, they kept the television cameras running. A live feed back to the camera trucks showed Bush vomiting on Japanese Prime Minister Kiichi Miyazawa and nearly passing out. The Japanese producers thought that the American president had suffered a heart attack—it was actually an attack of stomach flu—and they broadcast the footage live on Japanese television. To this day White House advancemen look through the preset cameras to make sure that they are turned off. That mistake will not be made again.

The wire photographers always arrived at the White House early and sat in the front row of the press briefing room having coffee and getting their equipment ready for the day. Bush would walk along the

President Bush receives a "photodog" hat from Bernie Boston during a photo op of a Bush staff meeting on February 14, 1989. Photo: Susan Biddle, The White House.

White House colonnade on his way to the Oval Office, make a right turn into the lower press office, and then open the door to the press room and ask, "How are you photodogs doing today?" Perhaps a few words about yesterday's events or past trips, then he was off to work. This happened regularly—until some reporters caught on, came to the White House earlier than their normal arrival times and started to ambush the president with questions.

Photographers were known to have great eyes, but their hearing and memory were not very good at all. At least that was the opinion of most reporters. Reporters would often come up to photographers after a photo session with the president and ask: "What did he say? Did he tell you this or that?" The photographers' reply was normally something like, "I didn't hear a thing. I was too busy making pictures. I can't remember." The photographers' access to presidents and other newsmakers depended on an old unwritten rule: "For the access of being in the room to make our pictures, what we hear stays with us. We are there to make pictures and that's it." Bush knew the unwritten rules and traditions of Washington well and knew that he could trust the photographers.

The president's love of his photodogs and the game of horse-shoes came together one Sunday morning. As Larry Downing, a for-

mer *Newsweek* staff photographer who went to work for Reuters, tells it, Bush telephoned photographer Doug Mills and asked him to put together a team to play against his team. With the match continuing late into the day, Bush's teammates began to disappear to do other things. The president turned to the White House butlers, still dressed in their server outfits, and ordered them to drop their trays and join his team's effort to defeat the photodogs.

Every year Bush would invite a few of the photodogs and their wives for a barbeque on the South Lawn. It was a small group of about forty people. In 1992, Bush took time out from the re-election campaign for the barbeque. Everyone knew that he was in the political fight of his life, and it looked like Democrat Bill Clinton was winning and Bush was losing. The president was rolling around the grass with his golden retriever Ranger and saying that we would come to the barbeque again next year.

The photographers were concerned that the gathering would never happen. And it did not.

Dirck Halstead takes a picture of President Bush with Raeanne Hytone at his annual barbeque for photographers on the South Lawn. Photo: Susan Biddle, The White House.

134

THE NEXT GENERATION

BILL CLINTON, GEORGE W. BUSH, BARACK OBAMA

Boston photographers got the first look at presidential candidates. Their bureaus assigned them to cover the candidates stumping through New Hampshire during the summer and fall before the

The Clintons and Gores on a campaign bus riding to the inaugural in Washington. Photo: Dennis Brack.

opening primaries. In 1991, Democratic candidate Bill Clinton, then the governor of Arkansas, was always available for pictures.

The photographers made pictures of Clinton prepping in a high school bathroom for a speech and of the candidate in behind-the-scenes hotel room staff meetings. They were his best buddies during the early campaign days. Pinochle was the card game of choice on the Clinton bus. At one time the governor amazed a photographer by reciting the cards the photographer had in his hand the last time they had played—three weeks before. As Clinton became more popular, however, the distance between the candidate and the news photographers widened and would never return to its more chummy days.

Candidate Clinton passing during an impromptu football game with the buddies in the press. Photo: Dennis Brack.

There was one exception: *Time* magazine. During the campaign photographer PF Bentley, on assignment for *Time* and working on a book, was granted the access the other photographers desired. After candidate Clinton became President Clinton, *Time* assigned Diana Walker of its Washington bureau for the special access that the *Time* editors requested. Walker, an extraordinary photographer, made good use of those moments. Her photographs became the classic images of the Clinton White House.

At the Democratic convention in 1996, Walker stood behind the curtains as the convention began to resonate with cheers for Clinton, who was seeking a second term. "I was standing by the entrance to the podium when suddenly President Clinton took this huge deep breath," Walker said. "I didn't realize I had the image until my great picture editor, Michele Stephenson, told me how the staff was so fascinated with this picture." As experienced a speaker as Clinton was, he still had to take a deep breath before going out on the stage.

On another *Time* assignment, Walker was in the White House on the day of Clinton's second inauguration, waiting for the family to leave for the festivities. Across the hall on the State Floor, Chelsea Clinton opened her coat to show her mother what she was wearing: a very short skirt. The first lady's body language made a caption for Walker's photograph totally unnecessary.

Bob McNeely was the official White House photographer for the first six years of the Clinton presidency. Although the official White House photographers had occasionally made their work available to the media in the past, the Clinton press office recognized the public relations value of the White House photo office work.

These releases were the beginning of a cascade of White House photos over the next two presidential administrations. The White House-released photographs were the source of many disagreements with the news photographers and the White House press office. The bond between the news photographers and the official photographers that had been made by David Hume Kennerly, Michael Evans,

White House handout photograph during Middle East peace negotiations.

137

and David Valdez began to fade.

Early in his presidency, Clinton attended one of the White House News Photographers Association's dinners. He could not wear a tux because of another event. As usual for this president, he was very late. In the Washington Hilton Hotel green room Clinton asked Ken Blaylock, the WHNPA president, and his official photographer, Bob McNeely,

Photojournalist Clinton and President Ken Blaylock at the White House News Photographers Association dinner in 1995. Photo: Mannie Garcia.

what he could do to make up for his later arrival and less-than-formal attire. McNeely took off his tan, safari-like photo vest and press tags

The Clintons happy. Photo: Dennis Brack.

and asked Clinton to take off his suit jacket and to put the vest and tags on. McNeely then gave Clinton his camera and told him to pretend to be snapping pictures of the WHNPA president as they walked to the podium. Clinton asked if there was any film in the camera and McNeely said no. Clinton said, "Put some damn film in this and I will take some pictures."

A "Voice of God" announcement over the sound system startled the crowd in the Hilton ballroom. "Ladies and gentlemen, the president." Yet, the Marine Band did not play "Ruffles and Flourishes," which usually precedes a presidential entry. WHNPA President Ken Blaylock walked onto the dais with a bevy of photographers walking backward and jockeying for the best position to make his picture—it was a real scrum. By the time Blaylock reached the podium the audience had recognized Clinton in the pack. Everyone roared with laughter. It was a nice touch for a very late speaker. By the way, the president's pictures were pretty good.

The Clintons sad. Photo: Dennis Brack.

The lack of behind-the-scenes access was not a big deal for the news photographers because there was much to see when Clinton and the first lady were before their lenses. Photographing the Clintons was like watching the characters in a Shakespearean play. Their emotions were captured by alert and skillful photographers. Some of these story-telling photographs could have been a reason that the Clintons kept the photographers at a distance, but one photograph caused a major skirmish.

In January 1998, the Clintons were on vacation in the United States Virgin Islands. The advance staff had marked off a section of the beach to give the Clintons privacy. Everyone knew the boundaries except the Clintons, and one morning they walked a little too far. Paul Richards of AFP and a few television crews were standing right where they were allowed to be. The surprised first couple made the best of an embarrassing situation with a little dance. The pictures of the Clintons in swimsuits got great play in the papers. Hillary Rodham Clinton was mad at the photographers. The Monica Lewinsky scandal was beginning to bloom at that time and the president thought that it would be a good idea to be mad at the photographers, too.

The Clintons together. Photo: Dennis Brack.

In the Clinton years, the press pool that accompanied the president consisted of two wire service reporters, three wire service photographers, one magazine photographer (rotating between *Time, Newsweek* and *U.S. News & World Report*), a television crew, a radio reporter, and two independent print reporters. Traveling everywhere with the president did not mean going in everywhere with the president.

For Clinton it meant rolling along in the presidential motorcade, stopping, and then waiting for hours. With Clinton the hours were long and the evenings often turned into the early mornings. The pool sat in the vehicles, usually large vans, and waited. The Watergate complex was back in the news as the home of Monica Lewinsky's mother. Photographers were staked out at several doors to watch for every move Lewinsky made. Stakeouts at the offices of independent counsel Ken Starr, the grand jury, and finally Capitol Hill during the impeachment process employed every photographer and technician in town. The money flowed for the crew members.

In times of war, presidents visit the troops. Abraham Lincoln traveled by steamer, then by horseback to visit the Army of the Potomac. Dwight D. Eisenhower flew to Korea. George H.W. Bush flew to Saudi Arabia during Operation Desert Storm. His son, President George W. Bush, wanted to visit the troops during the Iraq war. Everyone knew it would be a dangerous trip. Keeping the mission secret would be the key to survival in the days of surface to air missiles.

In 2003, Bush was having a quiet Thanksgiving vacation at his ranch in Waco, Texas. Brooks Kraft, *Time* magazine's White House photographer, was assured

On board Air Force One traveling to Baghdad. Photo: Chris Usher.

by his sources that absolutely nothing was going to happen, so he went home and freelancer Chris Usher was sent down to fill in on what was supposed to be a dull holiday weekend. The White House had decided to take all the photographers in Waco on the top-secret trip to Baghdad because they did not want those left behind asking questions when they could not find the other photographers. That could tip off the rest of the press corps and the secret would be out.

Early that Wednesday evening, the day before Thanksgiving, the White House advance staff contacted each photographer, with instructions to tell absolutely no one and meet at a nearby sports field. One photographer was missing—and that would not do. Cell phone calls to him went to voice mail. They waited as long as they could and then went by the press hotel. One photographer went in and banged on the missing photographer's door. Nothing. He turned and then decided to try one more time. He banged harder and the door finally opened and the groggy photographer appeared. He had just taken two sleeping pills. Told what was going on, he grabbed his gear and stumbled along.

The photographers and a few reporters, no television crew, got on a completely dark Air Force One with all of the window shades down. The plane lifted into the night from Waco and flew to Andrews Air Force Base in Maryland. With limited cabin lighting and the shades down, the plane landed and taxied straight into the giant hanger that houses the two Boeing 747 planes used by the president. The hanger doors rolled shut and the photographers got off the plane and walked over to the other—no pictures.

Bush was standing at the steps of the second plane. He did not say a word but put his finger to his mouth to warn them to keep quiet. A second motion by Bush signaled no cell phones, then a slashing motion across his throat made it all clear: Don't send any messages or there will be dire consequences. A television crew, additional reporters, and additional Secret Service agents were on the plane. The new Air Force One left the hanger in the dark and flew directly to the Baghdad airport.

The photographers were taken to a mess hall filled with soldiers who had been waiting for hours. As the photographers got into position they asked the soldiers near them what was going on. A soldier replied, "We're waiting for the Dallas Cowboys Cheerleaders." Paul Brenner, America's administrator in Iraq, told the troops that he was supposed to read the traditional Thanksgiving message from the president but that he would let another administration official do the honor.

Suddenly, Bush appeared. The place went wild. Later, the president served the Thanksgiving meal as the troops came through the mess line.

Everyone was worried about the take-off, the most dangerous part of the trip. The secret had held and Air Force One made an extremely steep take-off and raced to an altitude of 10,000 feet, the top range limit of stinger missiles.

The photographers did not always appreciate Bush's sense of humor. "Did you steal any of the silverware?" he asked some of the regulars on the days after the annual White House Christmas party for the press. The joking remark did not go over well the first time. The next year Bush said, "We want that silverware back." Every year the president asked the same demeaning question. In a similar vein, Bush had cute nicknames for some photographers. Charles Ommanney of *Newsweek* was "Chuckles." After the lights were called in the Cabinet

Charles Ommanney (checkered shirt) and Kevin Lamarque photograph President George W. Bush and UK Prime Minister Tony Blair in the Oval Office. Photo: Dennis Brack.

room, the president once yelled over to Ommanney: "When are you going to cut your hair?"

The photographers knew they had a friendship with Bush, just not the one that had with his father. In the Bush 43 years, the photographers were treated like reporters. They were people to be humored but kept at a distance. An attitude of arrogance by the head of the press advance contributed to the friction between the photographers and the presidential staff. The man was not very good at his job and quickly became the butt of the photographers' jokes.

Rick Friedman, a Boston photographer, kept his delightful positive attitude in even the most stressful situations. He was covering one of Bush's inaugurations and staying at another photographer's studio. It was well after midnight, the inaugural balls were finished, and Friedman headed to the studio. He reached into his tuxedo pants pocket for the studio key, but it was not there. No one was in the studio to answer the door and Friedman did not want to bother his host at such a late hour. Washington's Union Station was nearby, so he walked over and found a bench in the waiting room of the train station.

Friedman had his computer and began to edit and process his images of Inauguration Day. The other benches were occupied with homeless people who slept there on cold nights. Soon, one

Rick Friedman in his Union Station office. Credit: a homeless photo editor.

was looking over Friedman's shoulder, then another came up. Pretty soon more of the homeless joined them. All began offering their opinions on just which frame was better than the next. Friedman probably encouraged them, as was his way. It must have been a weird scene: a group of homeless people gathered around a tuxedo-clad man with laptop offering their opinions on which was the better picture of the president.

The Oval Office was silent as Bush watched Ben Bernanke raise his right his hand to take the oath of office as the chairman of the Board of Governors of the Federal Reserve System. CBS soundman Bob Bramson's brand-new cell phone started to ring. Knowing how much Bush detested cell phones ringing during his appearances, everyone cringed—everyone except Bramson. He had his headphones on and was listening to the microphone that he was holding on a ten-foot pole over his head. Someone tugged at Bramson and he caught on. The phone was ringing, Bush was glaring, Bernanke was taking the oath. The soundman held the pole in his right hand and fumbled around in his many pockets. The phone kept ringing. He found it and got it out of the pocket but, as luck would have it, he dropped it. The phone kept ringing, Bush kept glaring, Bernanke kept taking the oath. With the pole still high above his head, Bramson bent over, retrieved the phone, and flipped open the cover to silence the beast. The new phone was set to loud audio. Over Bernanke's oath, the audience heard: "Hey, Bramson, can you hear me? Are you good for a tee time at ten-thirty Saturday?" Bramson glanced at the president. "If looks could kill," he said later, "I'd be dead now."

There were two things about Bush that the photographers dearly loved. He did not go out in the evenings. The lid came over the White House intercom system right about five o'clock, meaning there would be no travel by the president. If there was an evening event, you could count on it being over by seven. And, second, he was always on time.

It had been forty years since small children had lived in the White House. Sasha and Malia Obama were cute kids and the media could not get enough coverage of them, but their parents were determined that their children would have a normal childhood. At least as normal as it could get when your father was the president of the United States. The photographers had worked well with Bill and Hillary Clinton with the understanding that they would cover their daughter, Chelsea, only when she was making news. It all worked pretty well.

Most likely President Barack Obama and his wife, Michelle, were expecting a battle with the photographers over coverage of their children. The battle never happened. The photographers—actually, the heads of the wire services, newspapers, and video bureaus—agreed to a simple rule: No one was to photograph the children without their parents. When the girls were in the same camera frame as their parents, they were fair game. No battles ensued, but there were many skirmishes. Times when Sasha and Malia came out to the South Lawn to watch their father return on Marine One set the president's press aides and the photographers into a fury. The children were definitely part of the story. For the most part the children were left alone. There

145

The Obamas light the National Christmas Tree; a photo that both Obamas and the press felt comfortable with publishing. Photo: Dennis Brack.

were no stakeouts at their schools as there had been with little Amy Carter in the seventies.

One major change for the photographers was the extremely early pool calls for the Obamas to travel to Sidwell Friends School for parent-teacher conferences. It was just a protective pool so there was no coverage, but it did not make those early calls less painful.

The rift between the photographers and the official White House photographers and the press office widened with the Obama administration's decision to take advantage of technology like Flickr to distribute the photographs made by the official photographers. Obama's official photographer, Pete Souza, was a member in good standing of the White House News Photographers Association before he took the job. In fact, Souza had been the chairman of the association's contest committee and was respected by all of the association's members as a first-rate photojournalist.

No one doubted Souza's integrity, but his photographs were being edited and released by the White House press office. The conflict had two parts. First, most were public relations photographs showing the Obamas at work, at play, and so on. The photographs were excellent. Perhaps it was the beautiful family, but the released pictures looked like the photographs used in banks or in soft drink advertisements. Second, by having official photographers take the pictures, the press office denied access to events that the press photogra-

Pete Souza at work in the East Room of the White House. Photo: Dennis Brack.

phers would normally have covered. Ron Edmonds, the senior White House photographer for the Associated Press during the first years of the Obama administration, made the policy of the photographers clear to the ever-changing series of press aides assigned to work with the photographers: If the photographers were allowed into an event, they were going to photograph everything that they saw.

The young men and women assigned to "handle the photographers" at the White House were on a constant rotation. Some moved on in the administration; some, thankfully, just went away; others got jobs in the media. New "photo wranglers" arrived and at first thought that their job was to direct the photographers on what pictures to make. Not for long. The wranglers found out what photographer James K. Atherton of the *Washington Post* would tell those at the White

Scottie Applewhite, AP focusing a remote camera before an appearance of President Obama in the press briefing room. The use of remote cameras thrived during the Obama years. Photographers were attempting to bring some life into the controlled and limited White House glimpses of the president.

House who did not like his photographs. "They don't pay me to make a picture that you like," he would say. "They pay me to make a picture that they like."

Obama was always polite when passing the photographers. There would be the quick "How you doing?" but never a pause to find out how they were actually doing. That was understandable because with any slight presidential pause, reporters would descend with a barrage of shouted questions. Yet some regarded Obama as being rather cool and aloof to the working men and women whom he saw every day. After all, the president did have more on his plate than chatting with the photographers. These were not the times of Harry S. Truman.

Not that a change in tone was beyond happening. On an overnight stop during the 2012 presidential campaign, photographers and crews covering Obama were told to come to a meeting room in the hotel and not to bring their cameras. The windows of the room were covered with paper. Inside were a couple of tubs of beer. The president came in and circulated from group to group talking about anything but politics. Most of the conversations were about sports and everyone was amazed at Obama's knowledge about all sports teams. The relaxed president talked to each group and seemed to enjoy the hour.

A new presidential administration did not mean new pranks among the photographers. In this case, the photographer was coming from the White House. He had worked all over the world, covering some dicey situations, but he had never covered Capitol Hill. As the newcomer walked into the office of the Senate Press Photographers Gallery on the third floor of the Capitol, the Hill photographers looked up and gasped. One told him, "You're pool on the floor of the Senate and you don't have a dark suit coat on!" A rush, a little search, and an old blue blazer was found. A bit large, but a fit. Now the directions: Down the elevator to the second floor, past the Senate men's room, and into the alcove next to the president's room. Tell them you are the pool photographer on the Senate floor today. Hurry—get going. The hardest part of giving the directions was keeping a straight face. The Senate had never allowed any photography in the chamber. The door-men stopped the photographer as he walked to the Senate floor. They were con-fused at first, listened to the photographer's announcement that he was the floor pool photographer for that day, and then they be-gan to smile.

Vice President Joe Biden was a sub-ject all to himself, fall-ing right into line with

President Obama and Vice President Biden share a joke in the State Dining Room of the White House. Photo: Dennis Brack.

the spicy, friendly vice presidents who preceded him. A United States senator since 1973, Biden had been a friend of the Washington pho-tographers for decades.

When he was chairman of the Senate Judiciary Committee, Biden presided over the confirmation hearings for Clarence Thomas, President George H.W. Bush's nominee to the Supreme Court in 1991. The hearings would break while the senators went to the Senate floor to vote and Biden would have to wait for his colleagues to re-turn. Often he would spend that time with the photographers, who were on the other side of the long table in the hearing room. One photographer commented on the massive amount of work at night that Biden had to do to prepare for the next day. Biden replied that he had prevailed on an endodontist to work late and he was undergoing a series of root canal operations. The Thomas hearings during the day and root canals at night—what a wonderful week for Joe Biden.

Photographers record Clarence Thomas being sworn in as a witness by Chairman Biden at the Thomas confirmation hearings to become an associate justice of the Supreme Court. Photo: Dennis Brack.

Once Biden started to tell a story, there would be no stopping him until he was finished. In an Oval Office photo op with Obama and a head of state, the photographers would be ushered in and the president and head of state would sit in the two chairs in front of the Oval Office fireplace and make their statements. Behind the line of camera crews and photographers the top administration officials would gather around the president's desk and wait for the press availability to end. During one of those press statements, as I was going around the back of the line of photographers, Biden signaled for me to come over. Then he began to tell a story to the secretary of state, Hillary Rodham Clinton.

Biden recalled how he had been a young unknown candidate for a Senate seat from Delaware. A *Time* magazine photographer—me—called with a request for a chance to photograph Biden shaking hands at a campaign rally. The person on the other end of the line was actually Biden's wife. As Biden told it, his wife cupped her hand over the phone and told him what *Time* wanted. Biden had never had a rally, but he told his wife to say there would be a rally at eleven Saturday morning at Delaware's Jones Beach. The Bidens started making signs and calling friends, telling them to come to Jones Beach, carry the signs, shout and wave and shake Biden's hand but not to let on that he was a friend. That Saturday, Biden shook hands at the rally and the photographer made his pictures. A flock of geese crossed the sky and—

splat!—a direct hit on the candidate— *splat!*—a direct hit on the photographer. They were the only two people to receive the geese's greetings. There was a message in there somewhere.

Vice President Biden tells his story about his geese greeting to Secretary of Defense Robert Gates. Photo: Dennis Brack.

The photo op ended and the press aides strongly encouraged the camera crews to leave the Oval Office. With me kneeling beside his chair, Biden approached the end of his story, but he was not finished. Obama looked over at his vice president and secretary of state as they laughed with the photographer. With a polite gesture, Biden told his boss that he would be finished in a minute.

HEROES

THE BEST IN THE BUSINESS

GEORGE TAMES

By his looks and dress you would never know that George Tames was the best Washington photographer of the twentieth century. A balding, elderly gentleman with a perennial smile, he would wear an old sport coat, dress shirt, and bow tie. As Woodrow "Woody" Wilson put it, Tames looked like your uncle or someone who sold you some-thing you liked. Within a couple of minutes, he would be telling you a joke, a new

George Tames at work in the Oval Office. Photo: Abbey Rowe, LOC.

joke, one that you had not heard. You would hear it again many times, but you would hear it for the first time from him.

While the photographers of the day carried two motor drives and a rangefinder around their necks, Tames used an aging Leica and a Nikon F with a High Point viewfinder—in chrome, no less. No self-respecting pro would use anything but black motor drive Nikons and never a High Point viewfinder. The equipment did not matter. Tames probably had made the picture of the day before his competitors came to work. If not, he would make it by the end of the day.

Tames would joke about his macho Greek heritage and all the pictures he just missed, but he did not miss many. The entree of being the staff photographer for the *New York Times Magazine* helped more than a little.

Covering Washington meant knowing what the story of the day was and then being there when it took place. When the major story was on Capitol Hill, Tames would start his day with breakfast in the Senate Dining Room with a senator who liked to hear the fresh jokes or perhaps the latest gossip. While sharing his stories Tames would get theirs. He would find out where the key senators were meeting and gently ask if he could drop by for a few minutes and take some pictures. It worked every time.

For years, Tames was the chairman of the White House News Photographers Association photographic contest committee. The association brought editors from throughout the nation to judge the contest. The night before the judging was a dinner, and Tames decided to entertain the judges at his home. Hanging on the walls were large prints of the photographs that he had entered in the contest the guests were judging the next day. The judges were not supposed to know the names of the photographers who had entered the contest. Well, they surely knew the pictures made by Tames.

The contest entries were not alone on the walls of the Tames home. There were photographs on every inch of every wall—his past prize-winning photos, photos of Tames at work, Tames with presidents and senators. Finally, at the top of the stairs there was one 5x7 photo of Tames and his wife, Franny. It was all about George. But his wife and children did not mind a bit—that was just George, and everyone loved him and his ego.

GEORGE HARRIS

President Theodore Roosevelt had a major impact on Washington photographic history. He encouraged George Harris to come to Washington and then helped Harris as he and his partner, Martha "Bunnie" Ewing, developed their business. Anyone taking the time to look at the tiny credits

George Harris at work in his studio. Credit: Harris & Ewing, LOC.

that appear with photographs from Washington would see that name an untold number of times: Harris & Ewing.

Harris was the photographer and Ewing the negative retoucher and studio manager. Together they created a news syndication and commercial photography business that became the largest photographic agency in Washington.

Harris began his career in Pittsburgh as a news photographer, and one of his first assignments was to cover the Johnstown flood in 1889. He moved to California and in 1902, while working for Hearst News Service in San Francisco, his managing editor told him about the need for news photos of senators and congressmen in Washington. Three years later he moved to Washington and opened Harris & Ewing Photographic News Service. Roosevelt was on hand for the opening.

President Theodore Roosevelt. Photo: George Harris. Credit: Library of Congress.

The president was not shy about offering advice to Harris. When the photographer said that he was not sure that he could take a photograph of the Cabinet in a tiny, dark room of the White House, Roosevelt roared: "Mr. Harris, I'm amazed. That's no kind of answer. When anybody asks if you can do anything in photography, tell them, 'Certainly I can.' Then find a way to do it." Harris made the photograph.

Harris was a good photographer, an exceptional portrait photographer, and a highly successful businessman. Harris & Ewing

The Roosevelt Cabinet by George Harris. Credit: Library of Congress.

thrived in the twenties and thirties when prints were delivered by train. However, the faster delivery of news photographs via wire photo signaled the beginning of the end for the company.

The Harris & Ewing sign remained above the door of 1335 F Street as a tribute to a Washington institution. Its legacy was preserved in the 700,000 negatives that Harris gave to the Library of Congress: portraits of leaders and ordinary people, pictures of natural disasters, marches, ships, machines and sporting events. It was a unique gift, a photographic history of the first half of the twentieth century.

Frank Cancellare

Everyone called him Cancy. A photographer for Acme News Pictures and later United Press International, Frank Cancellare became a legend in the world of wire service photographers. In his fifty-two years as a news photographer Cancy witnessed and photographed thousands of important events of the middle of the twentieth century.

After starting out as a "squeegee boy" in the darkroom at Acme News Pictures, Cancy photographed the height of the Depression in New York. He was transferred to Washington to photograph the Roosevelt administration. In World War II, his beat included China, Burma, and India and

Frank Cancellare along the Burma Road during World War II.

the activities of the Fifth and Sixth armies led by General Joseph W. "Vinegar Joe" Stillwell.

In covering the battles of the Chinese, British, and Americans against the Japanese for control of the Burma Road, Cancy spent months traveling by jeep and by foot. Later he was able to photograph a bombing raid on Yawata, the Japanese steel manufacturing center, from a B-29 Superfortress.

Then Cancy vanished. He was thought to have been killed or taken prisoner. Mysteriously he showed up in a hospital in Northern Australia and returned to Washington.

Cancy's photograph of President Harry S. Truman holding the issue of the *Chicago Tribune* inaccurately proclaiming "Dewey Defeats Truman" is a photographic icon, on permanent exhibit at the National Portrait Gallery in Washington. On that night in 1948, Byron "Beano" Rollins of the Associated Press, Al Muto of INP, and W. Eugene Smith with *Life* magazine made similar photographs, but Cancy's was the best.

Cancy covered Vice President Richard Nixon's "good will" trip to Venezuela in 1958. It was anything but a good-will trip. During a parade, the photographers were on a flatbed truck directly in front of Nixon's limousine. Toward the end of the parade, angry crowds surrounded both the truck and the limousine. Some photographers jumped off to make pictures in the midst of the melee, but Cancy stayed on the truck, watched the unfolding drama, and waited for the right moment. He had two film holders left—just four exposures—because it had been a long day of shooting. At the end of the riot, Cancy had made three perfectly exposed photographs of the peak of the action and came back to the hotel with one unexposed sheet of film. The remaining sheet was just in case something worse would happen.

Cancy held his reputation as being the best after United Press International absorbed Acme and assigned him to cover President Dwight D. Eisenhower and then President John F. Kennedy. Cancy was in the pool car in Dallas, Texas, on November 22, 1963. He jumped out of the car and made some of the few photographs of people reacting on Commerce Street seconds after the shots were fired.

When President Lyndon B. Johnson made a surprise visit to American troops at Vietnam's Cam Ranh Bay, Bill Snead was the local UPI photographer who handled Cancy's film. Snead remembered that Cancy had a shot of the president inspecting the troops and awarding soldiers their Purple Heart medals for their wounds. The brass needed a wounded man and one whom they selected turned out to be suffering from hemorrhoids. At the time, Snead hoped that the officials had given the man a bit of Preparation H along with the Purple Heart.

As Air Force One was flying over the United States, Cancy photographed President Richard M. Nixon and Soviet leader Leonid Brezhnev arm-wrestling. Naturally he was the prime photographer for UPI on Nixon's trip to China. Cancy's last trip on Air Force One came during the Carter administration. The president came back to the press section to wish Cancy farewell and safe travels in retirement.

In the wire service business you had to take the best pictures and do it without using much film. Film took time to develop and edit, and time was valuable. Cancy was the best when it came to working under the pressure of time. While other photographers would hand off packages with rolls of film, he would hand off an envelope with one roll and a scrawled note, "frame 16." There would be about twenty exposed frames on the roll and, sure enough, the best photograph would be in frame sixteen.

Cancy handed off a roll of 120 film and a roll of 35mm film to Frank Johnston during the coverage of Johnson at his ranch in Texas. Cancy told him to print frame one on the 35mm film and get in on the wire immediately and print the third frame on the 120 for the wire opener. Johnston found that Cancy's edit was right on.

Cancy used words like he used film. He did not say much, but when he did speak, the words would last in your mind. When the Nikon motor drive cameras came on the market, he said dismissively, "Motor drives— they make heroes out of bums." On another occasion he observed, "All you have to do to become famous in this town is to screw up!"

Frank Cancellare

As with many legendary characters, stories grew or were added to his accomplishments. White House photographers had fun telling this story, perhaps apocryphal, about Cancy on assignment. He was asked to make a portrait of one of the glamorous Gabor sisters at the Shoreham Hotel. Shortly after he entered the suite a tiny "yippie dog" began leaping and barking at his knees. His subject excused herself to touch up her make-up, leaving the yippie dog nipping and barking at Cancy. He saw a little ball and pitched it out an open door and on to the terrace. The ball rolled under the terrace railing and down twelve floors—and the dog followed.

Never one to waste film, Cancy turned the picture session into one of his shortest ever. As he was leaving he heard someone ask where the dog was. Cancy answered, "He's around here somewhere," and he was out the door.

CHARLIE TASNADI

"Compadre!" then an embrace or, at the very least, a hearty handshake. That was the way Charlie Tasnadi greeted his fellow photographers. He loved everything about his profession—especially his friends.

Perhaps Tasnadi's early years made him enjoy his life in Washington. In 1951 he and his wife crawled through a mine field on the Hungarian border and slipped under barbed wire to escape the communist rule. A guard with a machine gun saw them and turned the other way—and more than once. Tasnadi made that dangerous journey twice, the sec-

Charlie Tasnadi and his well-worn shoe at the National Press Club. Credit: WHNPA.

ond time returning with a child of a new friend. Thirty-eight years later Tasnadi returned to Hungary again, aboard Air Force One as a photographer covering President George H.W. Bush.

Toby Massey, the Washington photo bureau chief for the Associated Press, was confused when Tasnadi said no to a simple request. It came during a Republican Party convention. Ray Stubblebine had been working the AP long-lens position on the center camera stand all morning and needed a break. Tasnadi was working the floor when Massey yelled from the AP press desks next to the convention floor, "Spell Stubblebine." Tasnadi yelled back, "I can't." Massey pointed to the center camera stand and yelled, "Spell Stubblebine, up there." Frustrated, Tasnadi yelled back: "I can't spell Stubbelbine down here. What makes you think I can spell Stubblebine up there?"

Coming from Europe and South America, Tasnadi had never seen a baseball game. It was baseball season and the AP covered baseball. He arrived at the stadium and saw that baseball could be a difficult game to photograph. It seemed like all the action took place as the players slid into second base. Tasnadi wondered why the other photographers were not out there but figured that was their problem. At the start of the next inning Tasnadi walked out to second base and took a position that he thought would give him the perfect picture for one of those slides. Thousands of Washington Senators fans scratched their heads while the umpire explained that while it was probably the best place to make the picture, it was not going to happen.

Nothing could stand between Tasnadi and the picture he wanted to make. He was a big man and a gentleman who wore a coat and tie long after that dress was out of fashion, but he was a determined photographer-gentleman. Tasnadi liked to be walking backward directly in front of his president. More than once his bulldog tenacity paid off. When President Richard M. Nixon was shaking hands on a rope line in Brussels, Tasnadi was in position to catch that quick second where the president shook a well-wisher's hand while raising his other hand to take a look at his watch. It was one of Tasnadi's many prize-winning photographs.

Tasnadi's tenacity combined with the grace of a gentleman when he was one of two American photographers permitted into Cuba after decades of exclusion. Providing coverage of Senator George McGovern's visit in 1975 was the assignment, but the photographers also wanted to get a look at Cuban life, mainly the lack of groceries in the markets. The "minders" assigned to the photographers were, no doubt, under orders to not permit the photographers to go anywhere near the empty stores, but Tasnadi and I slipped away. The situation could have turned into an ugly incident, but it did not because Tasnadi talked to the minders in fluent Spanish when we surfaced. They were not happy, but they understood. It did help that Fidel Castro appeared the next day and we had news pictures to make. Tasnadi returned to Cuba many times over the years.

People loved Charlie Tasnadi and never laughed at him, even as they told stories about him. The AP photographer carried more cameras and lenses than anyone else in the hope of doing the best job possible. During the "arms for hostages" hearings known as Irangate, Tasnadi kept his camera bag right next to a network light stand. To give the bottom of the stand more stability the network electricians put small but heavy weights on the stand base. While Tasnadi was working on the other side of the Senate caucus room during the hearings, the photographers carefully removed the cameras and equipment in the bag and inserted one of the heavy weights. They placed Tasnadi's cameras on top, said nothing, and waited.

The hearing broke. Tasnadi picked up his bag, threw it over his shoulder, and was on his way. Later that afternoon, the photographers finally told him about his extra equipment. He laughed—as he always did.

JACKIE MARTIN

In President Calvin Coolidge's day and for many years to come, news photography was a man's world. Regardless, Jackie Martin wanted in and set about to prove herself.

In 1924 Martin was the news society editor at the news photography company Underwood & Underwood and, at night, the news society editor at the *Washington Times*. At the same time she had another job: coach of a woman's professional basketball team. She learned news photography, which meant learning how to hold steady for a very long exposure a heavy 5x7 Graflex camera loaded with a glass plate. Lessons in the dangers of flash powder were essential.

When the *Washington Herald* and the *Times* merged to become the *Washington Times Herald*, Martin was named the art director and picture editor. It was a first for a woman to hold those jobs on a large metropolitan newspaper. Martin took many of the photographic assignments that ranged from political conventions to sports.

Martin left the *Times Herald* in 1940 and the assignments began. One was very good—to illustrate a book on Brazilian aviation. She met with Brazilian President Getúlio Dornelles Vargas and then rode up the Amazon River on a Pan American flying boat. After that the planes got smaller and just a bit tricky.

It was a clear day so the fact the small Bellanca plane had no radio should not have been a problem. Even the high altitude to go over the Andes Mountains was not a problem until it began to get dark. The pilot thought that he had better land somewhere—anywhere. The entire town of Una, Brazil, watched as the little plane scraped along.

The undercarriage was torn off, the plane stayed upright and came to a halt. Martin found her camera and started taking pictures.

As a staff photographer for the *Chicago Sun* in 1942, Martin acquired another first: the first female photographer to be accepted for membership in the White House News Photographers Association.

Jackie Martin

World War II was the major story and Martin wanted a part of it. She accepted an assignment to photograph the Women's Army Auxiliary Corps, the WAACS, designed her own uniform, and was off to Fort Des Moines, Iowa, for photographs and training. The action was in Europe. In 1944 she obtained a contract with Macmillan Publishing to photograph a book on Army nurses. The assignment was in Italy, but the action was with the Seventh Army and the invasion of France—so much for the Macmillan contract. Martin spent six months with the Seventh Army, made more than four thousand photographs, and took extensive notes for a book.

She returned to Washington but soon was back in Europe to direct the Marshall Plan regional photographic operation. More awards and assignments followed. When her brother needed help, she became a vice president of Norwood Studios in Washington.

FRANCIS MILLER

He was the bad boy of the *Life* staff photographers, hired in the second group of photographers at the magazine, and seldom mentioned as one of the great *Life* photojournalists. Late in his long career he was assigned to Washington. The aristocratic editors at *Life* would probably like to forget all about Francis Miller because of his nickname: Nig. Yet this hefty white man with the eyebrow-raising nickname did more to help the civil rights movement than others.

In their prize-winning history of how the press covered the movement, Gene Roberts and Hank Klibanoff wrote: "*Life* magazine put together a team of three reporters and six photographers. Among the staff photographers was one legend, Francis Miller, whose nickname 'Nig' was especially unfortunate for a white man in the Deep South. Miller, who had been punched and taken into police custody while taking pictures in front of Central High in Little Rock, was a veteran newshound."

Francis Miller at work.

Miller took on the stories that the other *Life* photographers turned down. Many entailed sneaking pictures of the trumped-up trials of blacks and whites in the courtrooms of the South. He would dress in a suit and wear a wide tie. A tiny camera would be strapped around his waist with the lens fitted through a hole in the tie. He would sit in the second row of the visitor's section. At the right moment Miller would start coughing and then stand, allowing his camera a clear view of the court over the first row. Then he would make his pictures. Almost always the bailiffs caught on and escorted Miller out of the courtroom—and around to the back of the courthouse for a beating.

In the early sixties, Hank Suydam was the Washington bureau chief for *Life*. He and his wife were in the upper levels of Washington society and everyone in the bureau was thrilled, and a bit apprehensive, when they were invited to a formal dinner at the Suydam home as the venue for the annual Christmas party. Before becoming a photographer Miller and his wife had been circus performers. With a little prodding, Miller would perform some of his old circus tricks. At the formal dinner, Miller used a champagne flute to demonstrate the art of eating glass and later swallowed a flaming table knife.

Miller was never far from a libation. Assigned to join a Navy ship to cover the recovery of astronauts from a space mission, he brought two one-gallon containers. One held a brown liquid and was marked "developer" while the other held a clear liquid and was marked "hypo." The liquids looked like they could have been bourbon and gin—and they were.

A Navy ensign with a camera stood next to Miller as they waited for the astronauts' capsule and parachute to appear. The ensign had thought to tape two film cans to the straps of his camera and was pleased to see the famous *Life* photographer had done the same. Thinking he had the same idea as the real pro, the ensign watched as Miller unscrewed the top of one of his film cans, put it to his lips, and took a long gulp.

In the sixties, David Burnett and I were young photographers eager to learn the trade of photojournalism. The *Time/Life* bureau in Washington was the place to be if you wanted to learn from the best. *Life* editors would assign their greats to stories in Washington and they would congregate in the large bay for the photographers. Art Rickerby, Henry Groskinsky, Robert Phillips, and John Dominis would visit with their old friends Stan Wayman and Wally Bennett, and we loved every minute. One of the desks in the photographers' area belonged to Francis Miller and we loved to hear his stories as he fumbled through a locker filled with stuff that looked like it came from a poor yard sale: disguises, little cameras, large cameras, lots of strange aerial cameras, and cameras with motor drives long before Nikon had thought of them. Burnett and I both cherished the time spent in the *Time/Life* bureau, especially with Nig Miller, one of the great *Life* photographers.

Max Desfor

World War II turned out not to be Max Desfor's only war as a photographer. Five years after witnessing the surrender aboard the USS *Missouri*, he volunteered to return to Japan to help Charlie Gory in the AP's Tokyo bureau as the wire service covered the Korean War. The AP cabled an order that Desfor was not to go to Korea, but he said later that he never received the message.

Desfor was with a British unit when he heard about a parachute jump behind enemy lines to rescue Army prisoners of war on a train headed to North Korea. He borrowed a jeep and driver and headed for Tempo Air Force Base. When he got there he was told the mission was to take off at five-thirty the next morning. The supply officer gave him a parachute and rigged up a bag with a strap around his shoulder and down around his leg to hold his camera and gear. Desfor got on the plane with the soldiers—he thought of them as kids because they were so young, and they thought of him as an old man because he was in his early thirties.

As they were flying to the drop zone, the soldier next to Desfor asked if he had ever jumped before. Desfor told him he had not, and the soldiers advised him to bend his knees before he hit the ground. That was Desfor's only parachute training. The green light came on, Max made one frame, stuffed the camera in his bag, and jumped. About thirty seconds later, he hit the ground and immediately started making pictures. He had asked to be on the first wave of planes so he could make pictures of the second and third waves of paratroopers—and he did.

Max Desfor

Looking back, Desfor remembered making his best pictures when the North Korean army took the city of Pyongyang. To avoid being captured, he and his reporter got out of town and over the Yalu River in a jeep driven by a friend, a signal corps photographer. After they had crossed the river on a pontoon bridge, Desfor looked to his right and saw something that might make a photograph. The others wanted to keep going, but he insisted that they head to what they now could see was an old bridge covered with people. The bridge had been destroyed by bombing, yet people were crawling on what was left of the structure. Hundreds waited their turn to escape the North Korean army.

Desfor climbed up the ridge and found an overlook. He had to conserve his film, the slow Pan X film (100ASA), so he only made a few photographs in the freezing weather. He was using 4x5 film packs, which held twelve sheets of film and were less bulky than carrying 4x5 holders. When the Pulitzer Prize committee honored Desfor the following year, in 1951, it cited the image of the refugees fleeing across the battered bridge as "an outstanding example" of his photographic coverage of the Korean War.

Desfor worked in AP bureaus in Europe and the Far East and eventually made his way back to Washington, where he became the director of photography for *U.S. News and World Report*. In 2012 his friends joined him to celebrate his ninety-ninth birthday.

JAMES K. ATHERTON

"I was never a photojournalist. I was a news photographer." That was James K. Atherton's response to his introduction as the winner of the Lifetime Achievement Award at the White House News Photographers Association dinner in 1997. As his wife, Pat, remembered, "All the old guys in the crowd cheered."

For fifty years Jim Atherton made great pictures, first as a member of the Washington bureau of United Press International Washington in the sixties and later as the Capitol Hill photographer for the *Washington Post*. He and other UPI photographers—Ed Alley, Frank Cancellare, Maurice Johnston, and Stan Stearns—competed against double the number of photographers at the Associated Press. More often than not, however, the newspaper credits for Washington photographs would be UPI. They worked under the leadership of George Gaylin, a man everyone agreed was the worst manager they ever had. Yet Gaylin had the best eye in the business—he knew pictures.

Jim Atherton working on a different view during a JFK press conference held at the State Department auditorium. Credit: Courtesy Atherton family.

In 1963, the March on Washington, led by Martin Luther King Jr., was a major story. Gaylin had a special assignment for Atherton. The Lincoln Memorial was to be the focal point of the march. A few years before, using a forty-foot extension ladder held by four men, photographer George Tames had made a prize-winning picture from over Lincoln's shoulder for the *New York Times Magazine*. Gaylin wanted to try for something similar.

The week before the march Gaylin looked for a long bamboo pole and found what he thought would work. The problem was that it swayed back and forth when Gaylin and Atherton mounted a heavy Nikon motor drive with a 21mm lens to the top of the pole. A remote cord triggered the Nikon, but holding the pole was a two-man job. Atherton asked Stearns to help him. When they got to the Lincoln statue the AP photo team was there with a bright, shiny metal pole. Both made pictures and shipped their film. Gaylin said the film was all right, but Atherton was not satisfied. He went back to the memorial, put the rig together again, and asked a park ranger to help him hold the pole. It swayed back and forth, but Atherton made his photograph of the Lincoln statue, King, and the crowd filling the National Mall.

The *Washington Post* hired Atherton as its picture editor. After a few years behind the desk, he wanted back on the street and became the paper's photographer on Capitol Hill. The usually dull pictures of Hill activities came alive in his photographs. He appeared to be constantly on the wrong side of the light, but that was because he concentrated the shadows in his photographs and not the highlights. "You have to have shadows," he said. "They are important to show the features of a subject." When someone remarked that his photos of lawmakers and others on Capitol Hill looked posed, Atherton replied: "They're all posed. We don't tell them what to do. They come out and perform for us. The trick is to catch them when they are unaware of us and not posing."

Photographer David Burnett was amazed at how Atherton covered a committee hearing, even showing up well after the session had begun. "Just like the way that a sniper tracks his prey, he'd sit over on the side of the room for a while, and then once he'd figured it out, he'd take a leap, move this way or that way, and be done and out of the room before I could rewind my film. I would never have had the temerity to even think of standing next to him in a situation which didn't force it upon us.... I think I would have felt that was trespassing."

DAVE WIEGMAN

He was chosen for the ultimate press pool. During the height of the Cold War, Dave Wiegman of NBC and four other members of the White House press corps would go to "The Mountain" in the event of a nuclear attack. Safe in the bomb-proof bunker, Wiegman and UPI's Jim Atherton would document the president running the government while all of Washington and perhaps the entire nation suffered the nuclear might of the Soviet Union. Wiegman's first question to Pierre Salinger, President John F. Kennedy's press secretary: "What about our families?" The White House had no answer. Wiegman had one: He constructed an underground bomb shelter and stocked it with three months' worth of provisions.

A presidential trip Wiegman never forgot was Kennedy's visit to Dallas. The camera car in the motorcade stopped abruptly as the president's limousine rolled through Dealey Plaza. Wiegman knew something had happened but he did not know what or where so he put his Bell and Howell Filmo to his chest, turned it on, and just started running toward the front of the motorcade. He stopped to film people lying on the grass and then ran up toward the grassy knoll following Secret Service agent Lem Johns. Wiegman believed the camera records a thin wafer of time and did that day in Dallas.

Dave Wiegman in one of the many police vs press battles during Soviet Premier Nikita Khrushchev's visit to the United States.

Victories could be brief. In the process of shipping film, Wiegman left the makeshift press area at Parkland Hospital, where Kennedy had been taken, and came back to find the press buses had left. No cabs were to be found and Wiegman knew he was about to miss the swearing-in of Lyndon B. Johnson. As his blood pressure reached record levels, a lady pulled over her car, offered him a ride, and took him to the right gate at Love Field. He rushed to the press plane, joined the traveling press, and learned that there had been no television pictures of the swearing-in aboard Air Force One. Sometimes it was a great relief to hear those words—no coverage.

SHELLY FIELMAN

Friday, November 22, 1963, was Shelly Fielman's first day of work at NBC. He was assigned as a fourth man on the Bill Richards crew, which was covering Capitol Hill. It was a slow day and they thought that they would be able to go home early and just be on standby. They were having lunch at the Carroll Arms, a hotel next to the Dirksen Senate Office Building, when they heard the first news of the Kennedy shooting. Richards and crew rushed off leaving Fielman. He found a pay phone but had to look up the telephone number of the NBC bureau. The assignment desk sent him to National Airport to meet a messenger with a Nagra tape recorder, $5,000 in cash, and a ticket on an American Airlines flight to Dallas.

The Nagra tape recorder was a heavy, two-reel, quarter-inch tape machine that was the best sound recorder in the sixties, but it was a complicated machine even for experts. For Fielman, who had never laid eyes on the machine, it was a complete mystery. To make matters worse, the instructions on the Nagra were written in German. Fortunately one of the flight attendants spoke German and translated the labels. Fielman taped the English translations on the machine.

Fielman was paired with Henry Kokojan, the NBC cameraman for Dallas. Nothing excited Kokojan, who was used to covering the nasty news stories that were taking place in the South during the late fifties and sixties. He would film what is now called "B roll" or "cut-aways" and Fielman would record "wild sound" with the Nagra.

Two days after the assassination, Fielman and Kokojan were told to go to the Dallas police station for a "perp walk" with the suspected sniper, Lee Harvey Oswald. NBC had studio cameras in a fixed position in the underpass area of the police station, so Fielman and Kokojan were free to roam. In those days there was only a short microphone and Fielman had to stretch to get any sound when Oswald came out with his escort. Suddenly, nightclub owner Jack Ruby shot Oswald and chaos ensued. Fielman wondered just what kind of business he was getting into.

Fielman covered civil rights marches, war protests, and presidential campaigns, but the work he was most proud of were the few minutes he remained calm and got the pictures in the midst of the chaos on March 30, 1981. That day started as a slow one, too. Fielman was assigned Steve Caraway, a studio soundman out of the NBC studio. They were only covering the arrival and departure of President Ronald Reagan at the Washington Hilton. It was a pretty normal assignment and Fielman was looking forward to going for Mexican food for lunch.

As Reagan left the hotel John Hinkley Jr. lunged past Fielman and fired. Fielman kept a steady hand and followed the action and then looked for the gunman. He was the only cameraman who photographed Hinkley and the gun. It was quite an accomplishment because video journalists could only see half of what was going on around them. The view from the left was fine, but nothing could be seen to the right because the view was blocked by the camera.

Reagan's limousine roared off to the White House,

Shelly Fielman at the Tidal Basin on camera for a Today *show segment on the cherry blossoms. Photo: Hannah Kleber.*

173

then diverted to George Washington Hospital when the extent of Reagan's wound was known. Hinkley was arrested and all the injured were rushed to hospitals. After the video tape was shipped, Fielman's adrenalin level reached its end and he headed for a chair inside the Hilton. He looked over to Caraway, the soundman, and asked, "Did we get it?" He heard, "Yes, every second."

Fielman was honored with the White House News Photographers Association Lifetime Achievement Award. Not that his career was over. He continued covering the White House with the Obama administration.

DIRCK HALSTEAD

He insisted on flying first class and eating in the right places, with a glass of champagne if possible. He wore Gucci loafers, but not into a combat zone as some have suggested. Dirck Halstead took a great deal of kidding about his persona. He did pay attention to looking just how he wanted to look at all times, but then he gave a great deal of care to everything he did.

Part of the "Halstead persona" was being calm and cool at all times. He knew very little about Texas when he joined the UPI bureau in Dallas. In the morning paper the forecast warned of possible tornados, and Halstead thought, well, that was just what happens in Texas and began to prepare for his first afternoon shift. As he drove in, he noticed the clouds were dark and moving quickly, but he thought, well, that was how it must be in Texas. He strolled into the UPI photo bureau and casually asked, "What's new?" From under a desk, someone yelled, "We're in the middle of a tornado, you idiot!"

Quite often Halstead's attention to where he was and where he wanted to be resulted in being just a few steps ahead of other photographers. A decade before still photographers considered video, he had added a bulky video camera and a directional audio microphone to the still cameras he carried. Halstead was convinced that video and stills would blend and photojournalism was about storytelling with all types of equipment.

It took a couple of years, but the news business changed and photographers wanted to learn more about "convergence." Halstead began his Platypus workshops and converted the top photographers one by one: PF Bentley, Bill Gentile, twin brothers Peter and David Turnley, Maya Allenuzzo, Jim Sugar, Rick Smolan, Larry Price, David Leeson, and many more.

Dirck Halstead checks his equipment before boarding Time's *chartered Lear Jet in Havana, Cuba. Photo: Dennis Brack.*

In September 1997 Halstead started the website Digital Journalist in the hope that it would present individual photographs and picture essays in a fashion of *Life* magazine. The Digital Journalist became the bible of photographers.

Halstead was a journalist who used a camera. Research and creative anticipation with the experience of a veteran wire service photographer made him a valuable leader as the senior White House photographer for *Time*. He positioned his photographer troops and equipped them with the latest communications gear. Often this allowed *Time* to produce historic color photographic coverage in the early days of fast news magazine color closings. Using a camera extremely well, he had more *Time* covers than any other photographer in the history of the magazine.

Halstead covered his share of war stories. He was in Vietnam working for UPI and returned in 1975 as a *Time* photographer for the days before the Americans' quick exit from Saigon. In the summer of 1983, Halstead ran coverage of the siege of Beirut for *Time*, so he was well qualified to offer to young photographers who were off to cover wars. His best advice: Show me a photograph that would be worth your arm, your leg.

DIANA WALKER

When Gerald Ford was in the White House, Charlie Peters, editor-in-chief of the *Washington Monthly*, arranged for Diana Walker to have credentials to photograph for the *Monthly* on Capitol Hill and at the White House. She would shoot for the *Monthly*, sometimes "on spec," fill up a portfolio, and get on the next train to New York, visiting photo editors, some of whom began to assign her to this story or that. Eventually she connected with *Time*. Walker balanced her work and her life at home with two small boys and a most cooperative husband. Her hobby was turning into her profession.

Walker set out on a career of photographing people in Washington, on the Hill and in the White House—far, far away from sports and wars. "One thing I remember well from the great photographer-turned-picture editor of *People*, John Dominis," Walker said. "He might send this boarding school product to cover a party, but never up the mast of a twelve-meter schooner, as she wouldn't know what lens to take with her. He was right."

Time put Walker on contract in 1978. Soon, President Jimmy Carter was devoting himself almost entirely to obtaining the release of the Americans taken hostage in Iran. First lady Rosalynn

Diana Walker

Carter began to travel extensively for her husband, going abroad and visiting every state ahead of the 1980 presidential election. "I learned fast all about White House travel," she said. In 1984, she covered the presidential campaign of Democrat Walter Mondale.

Walker began covering the White House for *Time* on an every-other-month basis with photographer Dirck Halstead, from 1985 until 2001. "By then I felt I was done with a regular beat, but continued my relationship with *Time* right through Hillary Clinton's campaign," she said.

Gaining access to the president and the White House was often about establishing relationships. Walker often traveled with first lady Nancy Reagan during her husband's initial term. Slowly Walker developed a good working relationship with Mrs. Reagan's assistant, Elaine Crispin. Walker began to ask for some time behind the scenes and, over time, the press secretaries realized that they could trust her. During the Clinton years and into the presidential campaigns of Democrats Al Gore, John Kerry, and Hillary Rodham Clinton, Walker would continue to press for access.

"I made up my own rules for myself: that these behind-the-scenes ventures were for the photographer only," she remembered. "No reporters were to come along. I made up my mind I would never repeat to a journalist what I saw exactly, or more importantly, what was said while I was in the room." The rules were grounded in a basic truth: Walker never really heard conversation while concentrating on making a picture.

Getting to the president was usually a joint effort between the director of photography at *Time* and Walker with the press secretary. If successful, she would be attached to one of the White House staff photographers, going in and out of a situation with the staff photographer at the top of a meeting. Other times a press aide would take her in for a minute or two. "These quick moments with the president added up over a few days, with different activities each time I saw him," she said. "We usually would have enough for an interesting photo spread for the next week in *Time*."

Walker kept her equipment to a minimum on the days she was going inside. Her kit consisted of a safari-type jacket with deep pockets for film and camera batteries, enabling her to leave her camera bag on the floor and move around relatively unencumbered. She relied on quiet cameras with fast lenses—two Leica M6's, one with a 50mm lens and the other a 35mm. She always kept one Canon with a 24mm lens over her shoulder and a small 100mm in her pocket.

And she never used a flash, only fast black-and-white film (Tri-X at 800, or 3200 shot at 1600). Black-and-white film had a longer life from the standpoint of an archive. Most of all it signaled to readers that the pictures were different or somehow special—and exclusive. (She credited PF Bentley with pioneering the technique during the Clinton 1992 campaign.) She hardly spoke to the president or the first lady, except to say hello and only if spoken to. "Usually I was holding my breath," she recalled, "totally captivated by the scene in front of me, hoping to eek out a few more shots, a few more minutes."

In trying to obtain the behind-the-scenes access at the White House that *Time* sought, Walker found herself pursuing the most satisfying work of her career. "I of course realized the White House gave me access when it was advantageous for the president to be in *Time* magazine the following week," she said. "But I never passed up an opportunity to see a president off camera—or as close to off camera as one could get as a member of the press."

Her reward would come in witnessing small but special moments. "I remember particularly when I went into President Bush's cabin on Air Force One, this time in August of 1992," she said. "It was no quiet picture of him working as the plane taxied towards the gate in Houston and the awaiting conventioneers. Instead, as the president worked on his speech alone at his desk, totally concentrating on his work, Mrs. Bush was ready at the door, and son Marvin had his hands full with children careering about the cabin. It was a different and most human moment."

LARRY DOWNING

When Larry Downing worked a story every other photographer knew two things. First, they had better stand by for a practical joke. It could be just a *shhhh!* that brings an intimidated silence to the important people waiting for the president in the East Room. Or it could be part of an elaborate hoax that he had taken weeks to work, but it would come. Second, they will get beat by his photographs.

Larry was getting caption information from the toe marks at a NATO summit in 2004. President George W. Bush walked by and wanted to get his photograph made with world leader Larry Downing. The president did a little positioning, posed, and went on to meet with other world leaders. Photo: Charles Dharapak.

Downing was an intense competitor. He came to Washington working for UPI, became a *Newsweek* staff photographer, and later joined the Washington staff of Reuters. He took pride in saying that all he ever wanted to be was a "wire boy." An old school photojournalist, he knew that the caption was as important as the photograph. He would be right up front to make the picture—and with a sense of humor most of the time. At other times it took a little more, but Downing would get the picture, the best picture that there was to be made.

The White House assistant deputy press secretaries, the advance people, the photo wranglers—all the young men and women who attempted to tell the photographers what to do held that job for a very brief time. There were hundreds of them over the years. The ones that were good at the job were great friends of Downing. Both the photographers and the presidents realized that Downing was one of the people who brought a little life around the White House, making it a fun place to work.

WALLY MCNAMEE

For sixty years, the list of winners in the White House News Photographers Association contest have contained the name McNamee. Wally McNamee won the Photographer of the Year award four times. Like many photographers, he began his career as a copyboy, working for the *Washington Post*. He worked his way to the streets as a photographer and later became the *Newsweek* Washington bureau staff photographer. On major Washington stories, *Time* would hire every photographer in town, but it could not beat McNamee's talents: a great eye and an ability to anticipate where the action would take place.

Sometimes McNamee's dry wit was lost on his editors. President Richard Nixon's first trip as president was a European tour to meet various heads of state. The first stop was Belgium. Nixon shook hands with a crowd in downtown Brussels and the *Newsweek* photo team made pictures. It was high noon, but there was a slight drizzle and it was dark and gray. The exposure was 1/125 of a second at f/2.8 Ektachrome ASA 100, which was the fastest film available. This film had a bluish tint, which did not help matters. The film was shipped to New York and the next day McNamee called Bob Engle, the *Newsweek* cover editor, to check in. The pictures had been all right, but they were dark and gloomy. McNamee replied, "Well, we did have our gloom filters on." Engle shouted into the phone, "Take those gloom filters off immediately!" McNamee promised that he would.

At the news of the United States invasion of Grenada, the *Newsweek* Washington bureau called Pentagon public affairs and quickly realized that there would be no help in getting to the tiny island of Granada to cover the story. *Newsweek* decided to go aggressive, hired a jet, and assigned picture editor Jimmy Colton, staffer Wally McNamee and two freelance photographers to cover the story.

McNamee remembered what happened next:

Newsweek New York wired me $20,000. One of the freelancers, Jean-Louis Atlan, said that he had no money and I gave him $1,000. Atlan disappeared and returned with a box of cigars and a bottle of good Cognac. At that moment I knew we were on the right track.

The two guys flying our private jet were also Air National Guard. When we were over Grenada they contacted Grenada Air control, but were told to go away because this was a military-controlled area. The jet flew another hundred miles on to Barbados and landed. The team slept for a couple of hours. At dawn the jet flew to St. Vincent and dropped off Jean-Louis Atlan and me. We headed for the yacht club where we met an NBC crew where they were busy hiring a big sail-boat. They asked if we wanted to go in on the charter and I declined. These guys had cases of equipment and didn't look like they would be mobile and effective in a quick moving situation.

The NBC crew was still loading when a Boston Whaler showed up. We told the Whaler driver that we wanted to get to Grenada. He said that he would try but it would cost us. We settled on $10,000 to be paid in increments. Our first stop was Palm Island. The seas were six to eight feet. Atlan and I each had a rope attached to the forward part of the Whaler and we hung on as we bounced our way south-ward. Finally we got in the lee of the island where the waters were calm. At the end of the day we paid the Whaler driver $2,000 with the promise of the remainder when we reached Grenada. The only map of Grenada we had was a generic tourist map.

The next day we sped by the island of Carriacou, north of Grenada, and spotted the picket line of ships guarding the northern approach to the island. Our boat driver asked us what we wanted to do and at that precise moment a large naval ship dead ahead but some miles away started making smoke and moving in fast. I told the Whaler driver to head for the gap left by the departing ship and, by God, we went right through the picket line and soon were in the lee of Grenada and booking straight south doing forty miles per hour in flat seas.

With dead reckoning navigation our little boat landed on the beach of the Ramada Hotel in downtown St. George's, Grenada. The soldiers of the 82nd Airborne turned around to find Atlan and me at their backs. They were pissed. They leveled their weapons on us, told us to put up our hands. They wanted to know how we got there and ordered us to turn over our film. I told them that we wanted to see their CO.

The CO turned out to be Lt. Colonel "Mad Jack" Hamilton. Mad Jack laughed when we told him how we got there and said we could take all of the pictures that we wanted. The next day we pushed up the coast with the 82nd and were approached by a Marine sergeant who said he had a serious bitch with *Newsweek*. He had renewed his subscription and never received the pocket calculator he was promised. I said to the sergeant that we'd been looking for him everywhere and from my camera bag pulled out a *Newsweek* pocket calculator. I told him, "Here's your pocket calculator, thank you for your business and I am going to ask my photographer, Monsieur Atlan, to take a picture of the presentation, and please do not fail to renew your subscription when it expires." The sergeant stared at me and in true Marine Corps fashion responded, "I don't fucking believe this," and walked away—with his *Newsweek* calculator.

Wally McNamee. Photo: Nikki McNamee.

Toward the end of McNamee's career his son Win was taking his place as a prize-winning photo-journalist. Win first worked on the Reuters staff and became the senior staff photographer for Reuters. He was hired by Getty and became the top Getty photographer in Washington. Each year the list of White House News Photographers Association contest winners contains the name Win McNamee.

Wally McNamee recalled one of the thousands of Oval Office scrums he had joined. As usual the president was sitting on the chair

Win McNamee

on the right and the head of state was sitting on the left. It was an important visit, lots of photographers. The rush through the door from the South Lawn was vigorous and Wally did not fare well. The prime space was traditionally low and right in the middle. Wally was in the second tier and really pushing the photographer under him to get that just right low angle. Suddenly he got a mighty elbow jab from the photographer below. Wally looked down and realized the elbow belonged to Win.

Life goes on with Washington photographers.

CONCLUSION

SOMETIMES LIFE IS SWEET

Sweet time is the few minutes between dusk and total darkness. The structure of the buildings is visible, but all the imperfections in the scene are hidden in the shadows. There is a balance of the warm window light in the buildings and what is left of the sky is a

Sweet time at the White House. Photo: Dennis Brack.

rich blue with a magenta tint. It is a time to make photographs where everything is wonderful.

For photographers making pictures in Washington, sweet time can come during the pursuit of news or a great-looking picture. In some cases, it is just a matter of things working out far better than one could hope or imagine.

George Tames had a "sweet time" moment when he was taking an overall picture from the highest balcony of the Main Reading Room of the Library of Congress.

Just a slight brush of his elbow and there it went. The Leica 50mm lens was about the size of a half-roll of quarters, but to Tames it looked like a volley ball as it dropped from the balcony above the reading room. In what seemed like an eternity to Tames, the lens grew smaller and smaller and looked like it was going to hit a reader who was concentrating on his book. Tames leaned over the rail and prayed for a reprieve from his careless act.

Reading room Thomas Jefferson Building, Library of Congress. Photo: Dennis Brack.

Then he heard a tiny *clunk*. The reader continued to concentrate on his book. The lens had not even bounced. How had it not bounced? The lens was embedded in the wood of a table. Tames went down the stairs, picked up his well-dented lens, and walked out of the Library of Congress.

Tom Craven Sr. had a sweet moment on May 6, 1937. He was a rookie apprentice with the Paramount newsreel crew assigned to cover the evening arrival of the airship *Hindenburg* in Lakehurst, New Jersey. They set their camera in position

Tom Craven Sr. photographing the cherry blossoms in the sixties. Credit WHNPA.

and left Craven to watch the gear while they went to the bar. As the *Hindenburg* approached young Tom jumped up and turned on the camera—and ended up filming the explosion that sent the airship to the ground with a fiery crash.

Just as he turned the camera off, Craven realized he had forgotten to set the exposure. He looked and saw that the lens was set at the exposure for a daytime assignment that the crew had filmed earlier. He thought he had screwed up, but the daylight exposure was the perfect setting because of the brilliant light created by the explosion and fire. Three days later, Craven's work was on every movie theater newsreel and would become the historic footage of the *Hindenburg* explosion.

Tom Craven Sr. landed a job with Movietone News in Washington and was a favorite of President Dwight D. Eisenhower. His son, Tom Craven Jr., was a cameraman for CBS and made his own historic footage—from the Kennedy motorcade in Dallas on November 22, 1963.

Everyone liked Charlie Corte of United Press International, and he was a darned good photographer. Corte made some prize-winning photographs: President Harry S. Truman with actress Lauren Bacall on the piano at the National Press Club, President Dwight D. Eisenhower and Helen Keller.

In 1961, while returning from a trip to New York state, the Corte family was involved in a tragic car accident. Charlie Corte, his wife, and another family member died as a result of the accident. Their teenage daughter, Pattie, was paralyzed with a broken neck and their young son was injured.

The filming of Advise and Consent at the Sheraton Park (now the Wardman Marriott) at the White House News Photographers Association dinner. Credit: Harris & Ewing, Library of Congress.

Later that year the director Otto Preminger was in Washington filming the movie *Advise and Consent* and needed extras. Members of the White House News Photographers Association offered their help if Preminger would make a contribution to a fund for Pattie Corte. Preminger agreed and put $10,000 in the fund. Actor Charles Laughton starred in the movie, and he hit it off with the photographers. Perhaps it was their mutual admiration of bourbon.

Much of the filming took place at the Capitol, and a small room off the Rotunda was set aside for Laughton to rest between takes. At the end of the day the photographers and the actor finished their work with their mutual love for a good drink.

Preminger dedicated the profits earned from the premier of the film to Pattie Corte's fund. The premier, held in Washington, was quite a success and another $10,000 went into the fund. The money was enough to buy a small house equipped with special ramps for Pattie.

As plans for the funeral and burial of Senator Robert F. Kennedy were under discussion, officials contacted Bernie Roberts, for years an electrician for ABC News. Lighting Kennedy's burial ceremony at Arlington National Cemetery, the grave only steps from the grave of his brother, would be a challenge. The ceremony was planned for late afternoon and lighting might be needed for a brief time near its end.

The massive crowds along the funeral train route from New York to Washington delayed the start of the ceremony until late dusk. There was no power at the gravesite and Roberts had brought a large generator, the kind that is towed behind a truck. It had a full tank of fuel, which would have been adequate, but the lights had been on for hours and Roberts began to worry as the ceremony went on.

Then someone said, "Let's all light a candle." Scores of small flames lit up the scene. As the guests walked away from the burial site, the generator began to cough and gasp on the fuel's last fumes. And Bernie Roberts heaved a big sigh of relief.

John John, Caroline and Jacqueline Kennedy walking past the coffin of Robert Kennedy at Arlington National Cemetery. Photo: Dennis Brack.

British Prime Minister James Callaghan was facing a tough re-election in 1977 and needed all the help he could muster. The Economic Summit was scheduled for London and he thought that his role as a world leader would help his campaign.

The first summit meeting was held at Number 10 Downing Street. Callaghan came out of the famous Number 10 door to greet President Jimmy Carter. While he was waiting for the next head of state the prime minister strolled over to the photographers. They really needed a good picture for the next day's papers and told Callaghan that a group picture with the Number 10 Door as the background would be the picture of the summit. The photograph would get fantastic play in newspapers around the world.

Callaghan probably thought about the play in the British papers. "Tell you what," he said. "I'll raise it with the chaps." By chaps he meant the other heads of state. Callaghan went on to greet the heads of state and the photographers continued making a series of boring arrival pictures.

Shortly before the close of the meeting, Dick Keyser, the head of Carter's Secret Service detail, came out of Number 10 and glared

U.S. photographers await the decision by the chaps in front of Number 10 Downing Street.

across the street at the photographers. The head of French Prime Minister Valery Giscard d'Estaing's security detail was next to appear and glare at the photographers. The rest of the security teams appeared—as did more glares.

Finally, Callaghan and the other leaders came out. The photographers posed them right in front of the Number 10 door, but then the secretaries of state and treasury started through the door. A photographer shouted, "Get the underlings out of the picture." A poor choice of title, perhaps, but they got the message and filed back inside. The photographers needed the Number 10 on the door so someone shouted, "Close the door." The door was closed and the photographers got their picture.

With the arms-for-hostages scandal in full bloom in 1987, retired Air Force Major General Richard Secord was scheduled the following week to testify on sale of arms to Iran before a Senate panel. The editors of *Newsweek* wanted to run a photograph of Secord on the next week's cover, but the only picture available was a dated official photo when the retired general was still in the Air Force. *Newsweek* Washington staff photographers Wally McNamee and Larry Downing got the assignment.

Downing went to Secord's office in Tyson's Corner, Virginia, while McNamee went to Secord's house. And they waited. Suddenly, Secord rushed out of his house and climbed into his black Mercedes. McNamee did not get a picture, but he did jump in his own car and followed Secord. He called Downing and told him that the general was headed toward his office.

Sure enough, the black Mercedes arrived, braked quickly, and Secord was out and walking toward the office door. His hand appeared to be holding something in his suit pocket. Downing was right behind and called to the general. If Secord did not turn around, there would be no cover picture. And Secord would not look back.

Just as Secord reached the door, Downing politely called, "Sir, you dropped something." Secord felt his pocket and then turned to

JIM AND TAMMY
The Soap Opera Goes On

Newsweek
May 11, 1997 $2.00

THE SECORD STORY

A Close-Up Look at the First Witness in the Iran-Contra TV Hearings

Will He Link Reagan to the Conspiracy?

Maj. Gen. Richard V. Secord

look around. Downing had his finger on the Canon motor drive, the camera sung—*bap, bap, bap*—and he nailed the picture. Monday's *Newsweek* cover was Downing's picture of the general turning and looking for something that he had not dropped.

Discretion and the desire to keep at arm's length from the subjects sometimes gave way to the emotion of the moment. In 1998, President Bill Clinton and South African President Nelson Mandela were walking back to the entrance to the Cape Town prison where Mandela had been incarcerated for so many years. They stopped to allow the rest of their party to catch up. Then Clinton called over to photographer Diana Walker.

"I hesitated, and he gave me an encouraging wave," Walker said. "He began to introduce me to President Mandela. The president, as was his want, exaggerated mightily with his over-the-top description of my work … totally overblown but so nice."

Mandela took Walker's hand, and she stammered out that he was beloved by the world and that she had never been as honored to meet anyone. Mandela held her hand a moment longer and said, "Well, after that introduction by your president, I am not going to wash my hand all day!"

Malcolm Forbes steamed into Washington on his brand-new yacht, the *Highlander*. This was a very expensive ship complete with a Bell Jet Ranger Helicopter near the stern. The editors of *Time* thought that a picture of the millionaire and his latest toy would be perfect for the next week's People section. The assignment desk made an appointment for me through the Forbes public relations department for three in the afternoon.

The yacht was tied up at a pier. I just knew that the public re-lations person would produce Forbes at the gangplank and express his sorrow that I was able to photograph just a small portion of the ship—and with the afternoon sun shining directly into my lens. He would shake his head and say that Forbes was an extremely busy man and that was as good as it would get for me. The message would be: Work quickly and thanks for coming.

It was a clear day and the sun was perfect from the other side of the yacht. I arrived early, went past the *Highlander*, down to the pier to the dock of the old presidential yacht, *Sequoia*. I paid one of the deck hands fifty dollars to rent a dingy with a small power motor. My assis-tant and I climbed in and put-putted up to the stern of the *Highlander* a few minutes before three.

Fortunately, Forbes was alone and sitting on the stern deck. I got his attention, told him that I was the *Time* photographer he was waiting for, and explained that the best picture could be made from the river side of the ship. I asked him to join me on my yacht. He thought I was right and climbed down a small ladder and into the dingy.

We motored to the middle of the river and my assistant guided the dingy so that I was facing Forbes with the yacht as the background. I made pictures like mad—it was perfect, blue sky and the yacht.

As I was working I could see commotion on the deck of the *Highlander* as they searched for Forbes. Eventually they spotted him

Malcolm Forbes and his yacht The High-lander. Photo: Dennis Brack.

and the hand motions commenced. Since Forbes had his back to his yacht he was not aware of all of waving.

When I had made my pictures we chugged back to the *Highlander* and a reception of angry public relations and security men. Forbes did not care and turned to me and said, "Now that I've toured your yacht, I'd like to show you mine."

He took us around the ship and invited us to join him sometime on a cruise. The public relations people escorted us off the ship with an admonishment to always deal with them the next time. The picture ran large in the next week's issue of *Time*.

The day was over and it was time to travel home. Thoughts of pictures missed. Perhaps a smile, an inward smile, of course, about pictures made and not missed.

After a series of security checks, a walk up the steps of the world's largest and safest executive jet: Air Force One. The back steps, but what the heck. A right turn, then down the aisle to a large first-class seat. The camera straps went over the seat and all the equipment was stowed. No worries. There was plenty of room.

The only source of conflict might be which movies to watch in the cabin. It was a small skirmish with the reporters in the elite thirteen-member pool of journalists, but the photographers always ended up selecting the movie. Dinner was served by an Air Force steward shortly after takeoff. The chef had prepared the meal on a stove with fresh ingredients.

With a favorite drink in hand, the photographer looked out the window and thought, you know, this job is not so bad after all.

A LOOK AT
PHOTOGRAPHERS' TOOLS

Photographers love pictures first, but next they love the tools that make the pictures. In the United States, the story of the tools that make photography possible began with a tool of a different sort.

American inventor Samuel F. B. Morse traveled to Paris in 1839 to secure the French patents for his telegraph. On the boat, he learned of the photographic process created by Louis-Jacques-Mande' Daguerre. Since Morse's first love was painting, he was anxious to see Daguerre's pictures. Through the American consul in Paris, a meeting was arranged.

The Morse Telegraph key.

The First Camera.

The Morse Camera. Photo: Dennis Brack.

Daguerre invited Morse to visit his studio and laboratory and study his photographs. The next day Daguerre came to Morse and viewed his telegraph apparatus. Both men were impressed. At that moment Daguerre was obtaining a lifetime pension from the French government for his invention. He promised Morse that he would send him the plans and processing information when the pension was finalized. The information arrived later that year and Morse commissioned a cabinetmaker in Philadelphia to construct the first camera in the United States.

Today, this camera sits on the second shelf of Pod Two of the Smithsonian Institution warehouse in Suitland, Maryland.

WET PLATE PROCESS

Morse and his brothers soon switched to a process called wet plate collodion. The plate had to be wet with chemicals while the exposure was made and developed before it dried. The process was slow and only one image could be made and developed at a time.

A key ingredient was collodion, which was used to bind the image to the plate. Collodion came from dissolving guncotton, itself concentrated sulfuric and nitric acid, in ether and alcohol. In the wet plate process, collodion was poured over a glass plate in an even coating. In the dark, the plate was placed in a bath of silver nitrate to soak

Civil War photographer Rob Gibson making a picture of Senator Patrick Leahy using the wet plate collodion process. Photo: Dennis Brack

for a few minutes, then put into a light tight holder and quickly inserted in the camera. The dark slide of the holder was pulled and the lens cap removed for a brief time to allow the light to flow through the lens to the wet plate. With the lens cap reattached, the dark slide was be put back in. The holder was taken out of the camera and quickly brought back to the darkroom.

The plate was removed from the holder and placed in a developer solution of iron sulfate, acetic acid, and 190-proof grain alcohol. The development process was stopped by placing the plate in a water rinse, and fixed by dipping it in a potassium cyanide solution, a deadly chemical cocktail. Black stains from the silver nitrate were a common problem for early photographers, who often used cyanide to remove the stains from their hands.

There was nothing quick or candid about wet plate collodion photography. Photographers copied the poses of the portrait painters who went before them, and a smile was not considered to be proper or dignified. Yet there was also a technical reason. On a sunny day, the exposure could be as long as twenty seconds. A subject could not hold a smile for that amount of time without moving, which would

Clamp used to steady the subject's head during the long exposure.

The plate holder and dark slide.

Rob Gibson making a photograph by using the wet plate process. Photos: Dennis Brack.

cause the portrait to blur. Photographers traveled with clamps that were used to steady the subject's head during the exposure.

The Morse brothers taught about making photographs in their New York studio. One student was Mathew Brady, later famous for his photographs of the Civil War.

In the 1860's people purchased pocket-size albumen prints called "cartes de visite." These little prints gave Americans their first look at the leaders and generals of the conflict between the North and South. And, as historian s has noted, they provided a view of the horrors of war. Street hawkers sold them by the thousands on the streets of Washington and New York.

The essential ingredient for making these "cartes" was albumen, which is produced from egg whites and binds the photographic chemicals to the paper. T&E Anthony and Company, Mathew Brady's supplier, used 300,000 eggs a day at one point during the Civil War. Larger prints were exhibited in New York galleries, drawing huge crowds eager for news about the war.

From Wet Plates to Dry Plates

In the 1870's a process to affix a silver-bromide gelatin emulsion to a glass plate gave the photographer more flexibility. The need to coat the plates, rush to make the photograph, and then rush to develop the plate before it dried was eliminated. With the dry plate process came an increase of the speed of the emulsions, which allowed photographers to hold their cameras by hand instead of mounted on a stand.

A myriad of new cameras were invented. The most popular was the "Detective Camera," which was no more than a lens with a shutter in a

Detective Camera. D.B. Collection.

light-proof box (usually leather-coated), which would hold several glass plate holders. The operator could make pictures without the subject knowing that he or she was being photographed. Candid photography was born.

Making photographs became easier still in 1872 with the invention of celluloid, a flexible material that replaced the rigid glass plates. In the next ten years celluloid backing would be improved and then used in small roll film cameras and moving pictures. The professionals still liked the large cameras and their 8x10 or 5x7 plates.

SEARCHING FOR GOOD LIGHT

The right light was always the key ingredient to making good photographs. In the first days of photography, the blue hue of the north light was thought to be the best.

Harry Van Tine and Joe Johnson, The National Photo Company.

Wet and dry plates responded to cold blue light (6,700 Kelvin or higher) and it was thought that the North light was the best source. In fact, the warmer light would not register on the plates at all. A glass plate coated with red dye was in the ceiling of photographers' pro-

Mathew Brady's studio.
Photo: Dennis Brack.

cessing wagons and studios. At one point in the developing process this light could be used to allow the processor some light to work with. A warm, yellowish red light is used today in labs making gelatin silver prints.

The first studios were built with large skylights facing north. The skylight of Mathew Brady's studio in Washington faced north—and it still does, though it is not open to the public. A few steps north from Pennsylvania Avenue NW on Seventh Street NW are the twin spires of what is now the headquarters of the National Council of Negro Women. Brady's skylight can be seen at the top of the third building of this structure.

The sun changes position during the year, which cost the studios their good light during some months. Thomas Alva

Photo: Dennis Brack.

Edison had a solution. In 1893 he built a photographic studio on a pivot, allowing it to be turned for the light that he wanted.

ALONG CAME FRED AND THE HALFTONE

Important pictures were being made during the second half of the nineteenth century. The railroad photographers like Andrew Joseph Russell and Charles Roscoe Savage recorded the construction of the Union Pacific and Central Pacific and the movement to the West. Both of these photographers made the historic photograph of the laying of the Golden Spike at Promontory Point, Utah. Eadweard Muybridge's experiments brought motion to still photographs with his racing horse series named "Sallie Gardner at a Gallop." Muybridge's murals documented the grandeur of Yosemite. Thousands of photographers with studios preserved the images of national leaders and ordinary families for future generations to enjoy.

Great photographs, but only a handful of people were able to view them. Few photographs were printed in newspapers because there were no good-quality and efficient means of reproducing the images. The photograph would have to be crafted into a wood-based engraving, a process that took time and skill. The result was a harsh, black-on-white image that looked like an etching—not a photograph.

Then Frederic Eugene Ives had an idea. In 1875, the very young head of the photographic laboratory at Cornell University figured out how to break down a photographic image into thousands of dots that could be translated into various shades. The result was a printed image that had detail in the shadow and highlight areas—the halftone process. Over the next three decades the process would improve and more and more newspapers would use photographs for their primary illustrations. And papers began to hire news photographers.

Harris & Ewing. Credit: Library of Congress.

HEAVY LIFTING

Imagine carrying ten windowpanes around all day. Each windowpane would be stored in a sturdy, lightproof wood box—and that would be just the film. In another box would be a twelve-pound camera, one made of wood and covered with leather, approximately thirteen inches tall, nine inches wide, and ten inches deep.

The camera box contained a movable mirror set at a forty-five-degree angle. When in the down position the mirror reflected the image from the lens upward to a ground glass so that the photographer could focus by looking down through the hood at the top of the box. At the back of the box was a curtain of thin, lightproof black cloth wound on two rolls. One roll was at the top of the box, the other roll at the bottom of the box. The curtain had a slit in the middle to allow the light to travel through and give just the right amount of light to expose the glass plate or film at the far end of the box.

Credit: D.B.Collection.

The curtain was wound up to the top roll so that a black part of the curtain would block the light from the glass plate. Triggering the spring controlling these two rolls made the curtain travel down to the bottom roll. As it traveled down the slit in the curtain exposed the glass plate and then another part of the curtain blocked the glass plate from any additional light. The truth be known, there were many slits and black areas on the fine cloth roll to make different exposure lengths—it was complicated. Basically it was a focal plane shutter much like those used in single lens reflex film cameras.

To make a photograph, the photographer had to wind the curtain to the proper position, place the film holder in the camera, pull slide on the holder, place the slide out of the way, focus the camera, push a latch that will raise the mirror up to the viewing screen, hold the camera very steady, and push another latch to release the shutter curtain. The speed of the glass plates was very slow (about 25 ASA) so even on a sunny day the exposure was about a 60th to a 125th of a second.

Photographers at the Polo Grounds. Credit: Library of Congress.

Impossible? Photographers did make pictures. And they dressed in suits and derby hats.

THE WIRE

For the first thirty years of the twentieth century, the news picture agencies made multiple sets of 8x10 silver nitrate prints of images in Washington and put the prints into envelopes. A messenger rushed to Union Station with a pocketful of five-dollar bills. He found the chief conductors of the trains to New York, Chicago, and other major cities and handed the conductors the envelope and a five-dollar bill. He reminded the conductor of the five-dollar bill that he would receive when he handed the envelope to a messenger in the other city. Those messengers rushed the envelopes to the newspapers, and the photographs became half tones on the front pages.

AT&T revolutionized the news picture business in 1935. Its lab

News pictures rolling off of a United Press International terminal at Channel Nine in Washington, D.C. Photo: Dennis Brack.

had spent a fortune on producing an invention to transmit images by wire. A photographic image was broken down into a series of fine lines. A print was attached to a cylinder, the cylinder rotated, and a beam of light scanned each line. The light reflected the density of each piece of the photograph in that tiny line. This electronic tonal value could then be transmitted on a telephone line.

The Associated Press was the first to transmit images and ordered telephone lines dedicated to wiring photo transmissions. International News Photos and the other large syndicates soon followed. The smaller local companies such as Harris and Ewing and Brown Brothers could not compete and were left to selling stock pictures and producing feature picture packages.

Let There Be Light

When ignited, magnesium creates a brilliant light for an instant. That was just what photographers needed to make their photographs in dark places. With the flash powder gun, a very small amount of magnesium would be sprinkled into the tray of the powder gun. The person holding the flash powder gun ignited the magnesium powder by making a spark with a flint mechanism in the handle that worked much like a cigarette lighter. The photographer opened the shutter of his camera, fired the flash powder gun, and closed the shutter.

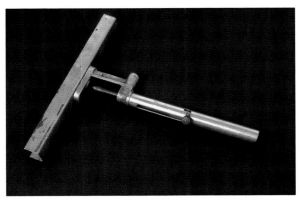

Sometimes this process would work and create a blinding light followed by a dense cloud of dust that covered everything. Even if everything went well, the smoke was a problem. Photographer Ike

The John Marshall model Meteor Model A Flashpowder Gun. Photo: Dennis Brack.

Pridgeon recalled, "We were always in a tizzy about the danger of the stuff exploding and about the quantity of the powder to be used."

Sometimes things did not go well. Harry Mellon Rhoads of the *Rocky Mountain News* always added just a bit of gunpowder to his magnesium to give it a little more zip. He was sent to photograph the ballroom of a newly built hotel. He burned the building to the ground. Rhoads had no eyebrows and whenever he went to photograph any large public gathering he was trailed by a fireman carrying a fire extinguisher.

A story often told about the days of flash powder began with a feature assignment on a Washington socialite and her prized canary. The lady was positioned right next to the cage with her best smile. The photographer waited until the canary got into just the right place and triggered his flashgun. The magnesium flash powder ignited and created a blast of brilliant light. The canary dropped dead from the swing in the cage. A heart attack? The photographer did not wait to find out. He quickly gathered his equipment and told the crying socialite as he left, "Lady, I'll send you a picture."

A photographer assigned to photograph a prizefight at the City Club on G Street had a similar impact on his subjects. When he fired his flashgun, the favorite in the bout was momentarily blinded. The underdog knocked him out. The photographer, hauling his camera and tripod and other gear, fled down a fire escape as a mob pursued him.

Occasionally a photographer would not wait for the tray of the flash powder gun to cool before pouring in new magnesium for the next photograph. *Bam!* An unexpected explosion. Photographer Woodrow "Woody" Wilson said, "You'd be surprised, how many photographers had fingers missing."

After flash bulbs replaced flash powder, one photographer in New York City kept lighting up the magne-

Weegee

sium: Arthur Fellig, best known as Weegee. A freelancer who specialized in crime coverage, he had no problem using flash powder. When covering a fire, other photographers would wait for Weegee. He would prepare to make a picture, shout "open shutter" and ignite the powder. Herb Schwartz, then a young still photographer and later a top CBS video journalist, remembered Weegee placing his flash a bit too close to a window. The vibration broke the glass.

THE VACUBLITZ ARRIVES

The flashbulb, invented in Germany in 1931 and called the

Vacublitz, changed the business. The first was the size of a sixty-watt light bulb and had the same screw in base of a regular light bulb. It was frightfully expensive.

The flash bulbs were thin wires and magnesium, vacuum-packed in a light bulb housing that could be triggered by even the slightest electrical charge. Many a photographer who put several bulbs in his pocket would be jolted by an explosion because of the static electricity in his pants. In New York, photographers carefully planned their subway route to avoid the subway power terminals.

Photo: Dennis Brack.

The new technology gave rise to new stories. A wedding photographer budgeted five bulbs to cover a wedding. When he realized the next day that he only used four of the five, he went back to the church to retrieve the fifth. He noticed that the priest's right hand was bandaged. "Funny thing," the priest said, "I was screwing this light bulb into a socket and it blew up in my hand." The priest asked the photographer what had brought him back to the church. The photographer quickly replied, "The morning Mass."

At first the new flashbulbs were warmly greeted at the White House because there was no noise and no smoke. Two photographers used them at a ceremony and afterwards President Franklin D. Roosevelt came over and asked, "Is that a new one?" But the warm greeting was short-lived. The flashes hurt the president's eyes and an order came down from press secretary Steve Early: The pictures would be made only when he said "shoot."

In a Senate hearing chaired by Senator Tom Connally, the photographers crowded around a witness and fired away with flashbulbs. Finally the witness complained to Connally. With a cigar in his hand, the chairman waved at the photographers and said, "You can click, but you can't bulb!"

FARBER'S GREAT INVENTION

The *Milwaukee Journal* was a newspaper that attracted the best photographers. Its editors appreciated good pictures and played individual photos and picture stories well. Talented photographers like Howard Sochurek and the Scherschel brothers made the *Milwaukee Journal* the spawning ground for leading photojournalists. One of them, Edward Farber, was looking for a portable light source with a brief flash duration that would freeze sports action. In the early 1940's he invented a thirteen-pound unit that he called the "stroboflash." Over the years it evolved into the Stroboflash II, which became the standard for newspaper photographers throughout the United States in the fifties.

Soon the stroboflash had competitors. Some were dangerous, but the Megaloon took the prize. This monster was a heavy wet cell unit, sort of like a car battery. The side of the battery pack had an opening that allowed the photographer to see the little red and white balls that indicated how many flashes he had left. It really did not matter because the unit could quit at any time. It seemed to be able to smell a good picture about to happen and stop working immediately. The Megaloon also loved moisture because it was a good opportunity to shock the devil out of the photographer. On the wet grass of a football field sideline at night, it was not uncommon to see a photographer hustling down the sideline to get in position for the next play and then jump about five feet when he received a blessing from his Megaloon strobe.

In spite of the rough beginning, the electronic flash or strobe became many a photographer's best friend. The big faulty units slimmed down to standards like the Heiland's, the wire service photographers' favorite, and the Mighty Lite, the favorite of the magazine shooters. Those units had competition with the new cameras, fast films, and the growing popularity of available light photography. Some photographers like John Mazziotta of the *Dallas Morning News* were loyal to the strobe units. When asked about shooting available light, Mazziotta would say that he always used available light, then tap the head of his Heiland strobe and add, "My light is right here and it is always available."

Another favorite strobe was the Metz, large and extremely powerful with a big head on a large, long handle. Photographers called them "potato mashers." In London, "Jumping John" Johnny Rex carried the largest of the potato mashers and pasted little signs over the controls. On the low power setting he pasted "stun" and over the high setting he pasted "kill." His negatives were fun to see. The first frame of a series would show the subject would be smiling, but the second showed the subject wiping his eyes or wincing.

Life magazine and the *Saturday Evening Post* owned the state-of-the-art Ascors. The units were about the size of a small washing machine, and they were dangerous. They would shock you in a fraction of a second. The only people who were allowed to touch them were the assistants. There were always two or more assistants and each assistant had a rope tied around his waist. If an assistant did receive a shock, he would stick to the unit. The other assistant would grab the rope, which did not conduct electricity, and pull the first assistant to safety.

THE SPEED GRAPHIC

George Eastman purchased Folmer and Schwing Manufacturing, a bicycle company that also made cameras, in 1905. Such a combination of products was not uncommon at that time. The 4x5 Speed Graphic camera was introduced in 1912. The camera contained a cloth curtain focal plane shutter and rail-based bellows mounted on a carriage that could be folded into a tight box. Improvements, such as a front leaf shutter and a sports finder, were added over the years, but the basic camera design never changed. In 1947 the company came out with the Pacemaker Graphic, which was the same camera without the focal plane shutter.

The 4x5 Speed Graphic was the sweetheart of press photographers for sixty years. At one time sixteen of the twenty Pulitzer Prize-winning photographs were made with this bulky but durable picture-making machine. The Speed Graphic became the identifying symbol of the news photographer.

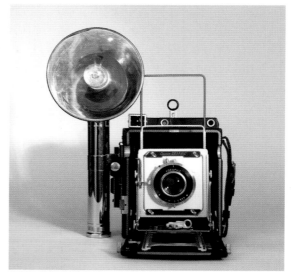

4x5 Crown Graphic. Credit: D.B. Collection.

The film was put into the back of the Speed Graphic with film holders and a slide would be pulled, much like the film holders in the Wet Plate Process. A photographer started the day with about ten film holders, each containing two sheets of film. Usually a photographer carried the holder in the camera and perhaps one holder in each coat pocket. Every exposure was important. The first thing that a press photographer would look for in a news situation was one good picture that would tell the story. It was called "making one for the bag." Once the photographer had that one picture, he could relax, look for something new, perhaps a feature picture, but he had to have that "one for the bag" before he did anything.

Times changed. The Rolleiflexs, Nikons, and Leicas became news photographers' symbols and sweethearts. In 1966 the Graflex division of Eastman Kodak was sold to the Singer Corporation, which had no interest in continuing to make cameras. The Speed Graphic production lines slowed and then stopped.

Abe Jenkin's Rollei

Most photographers looked down into the top of the Rolleiflex, took their time, and focused. Washington news photographers used the camera in a different manner. The first stop for a Washington photographer with a new Rollei would be Abe Jenkin's house. A printer at the Associated Press,

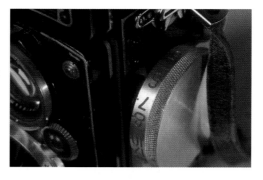

Jenkin would take the camera, walk down the stairs to a cluttered basement workshop, and start talking while he turned the camera into a news picture-making machine. First, he modified the top focus hood to make way for a sturdy sports finder. Then he replaced the focusing device on the camera with a large knob that showed the distance in feet. The knob had numbers six, eight, ten, to double zero engraved on it, which could be lined up with a precisely calibrated arrow.

When the number six was matched to the arrow, the subject six feet away from the camera was in perfect focus. A good news photographer knew how to judge focus distance, and the reference number was enough. Newspaper and wire service photographers used the Rollei for about ten years starting about 1957.

LEICAS AND NIKONS

Well before the debut of *Life* magazine in 1936, German illustrated magazines flourished. *Berliner Illustrirte Zeitung* and *Biz* had more than two million readers. They were popular because of a new style of candid photography and a new form of storytelling: the photo essay.

Leica M4. Credit: D.B. Collection.

German photographers like Alfred Eisenstaedt, Fritz Goro, and Walter Sanders had mastered the art of making photographs in the candid style that the *Life* editors were searching for. They came to the United States and *Life* gave them assignments and later staff positions. Their camera of choice was the Leica F2. While some photographers used the Zeiss Contax, the Leica was the camera for 35mm journalism. They were quiet and good for photographers working with short lenses (21mm, 35mm, and 50mm) and perfect for reportage journalism.

The Nikon F with a motordrive and a Jacobs Remo battery pack—the must camera for the press photographer in the sixties. Credit: D.B. Collection.

In the fifties Max Desfor, the Associated Press photographer in Japan, and photographer David Douglas Duncan took a tour of the Nikon Tokyo plant. They watched the workers pick up the boxes of the part that each was tasked to install on the Nikon S chassis that moved down the conveyer belt in the middle of the two lines of workers. Duncan purchased a Nikon S rangefinder camera and then another. The Nikon reputation grew.

In 1959 Nikon introduced the Nikon F, a single lens reflex camera. It was a durable camera that allowed the photographer to use long lenses. During the sixties a rangefinder Nikon S or SP or a Leica and the Nikon F and 35mm film became the preferred tools of the news photographer. Maurice Sorrell, the *Ebony* photographer who covered the civil rights marches then, was buried with a roll of Tri-X in his pocket.

LIGHT FROM THE SCOOPS

The opportunities for making pictures in the Oval Office and the Cabinet Room—photo opps—have been illuminated by the same knicked up, bent up, old "scoop" lamps held by a series of colorful fellows for at least sixty years. The most colorful of these "electricians" was Cleve Ryan, a wonderful little Irishman filled with charm and mischief.

Photo: Abbie Rowe, Department of Interior.

Ryan was just there at the White House, employed by no one but paid by everyone. He could be very helpful. He knew everything that was going on and would share his information with his friends, who would quietly slip at least a fifty-dollar bill to him at the end of a presidential trip. Ryan knew that the money was coming out of expense accounts and he did not mind graciously accepting it. You never knew when you would need his help.

Ryan was called the "Postmaster" because he was always hitting on presidents to make him a postmaster. He was sure that his best chance for the job was with President John F. Kennedy and dreamed of being the postmaster of Gloucester, Massachusetts. Ryan was on the floor of the Oval Office plugging in his lights while Kennedy

President Lyndon Baines Johnson meeting with black leaders in the White House Cabinet Room three days after the assassination of Dr. Martin Luther King Jr. Photo: Dennis Brack.

worked at his desk. The president stopped his work and asked, "Cleve, how long did it take you to learn your job?" Ryan looked up, thought a bit, and replied, "About ten minutes."

There was a time when Ryan thought that he had lost his job. The press office of the Nixon administration renamed many things to put a positive spin on everything. In the press schedules the name electrician was

President Carter congratulating Cleve on his last day as the White House electrician. Photo: Dennis Brack.

changed to "illumination engineer." As photographer George Tames remembered, "When the news press types shouted for the photographers to make way for the illumination engineer, Cleve Ryan yelled out, 'Who got my job?'"

Ryan never received his postmaster appointment, but he did

get a nice little photo opp in the Oval Office with President Jimmy Carter lit by the ancient "scoops." New models had been tested over the years, but everyone liked the wide, even light they provided. The bulbs have changed and the wiring has been updated, but the scoops may be the only thing that has not changed in White House press coverage since the Truman administration.

One man who held the scoops can not be omitted from this book: Marvin Purbaugh, the NBC electrician. Many news magazine covers were the result of Marvin Purbaugh's excellent lighting. Photo: Dennis Brack.

In recent years, the major networks, in an effort to reduce costs, cut out the job of a network pool electrician. The scoops were relegated to a rack next to the photographers' ladders in the press work area, brought out only occasionally.

The Big Men

During the last months of the Nixon administration and the first years of the Ford administrations, network news coverage underwent a major transition. On-location news coverage changed from 16mm film to videotape. Since motion picture news coverage grew out of the old movie theater newsreels, which used 35mm motion picture film, the sound men, cameramen, and grips were all union members. It was a tight union and you almost had to be a son of a member to be allowed to join the union and cover the news for the networks using a film camera. That union had the opportunity to retrain their members and transition into video, but they declined—a bad decision. The networks acted quickly to encourage enrollment in another union that would be more sympathetic to their needs. The network management could hire the men they wanted, and they did.

At that time presidential trips were always the major story of the day and suddenly, some very big men came onto the press planes with equipment that made the 16mm film cameras look like toys. These fellows were not only big, but also hostile and aggressive. It was said that many were former professional football linemen—good football players or not, they were huge and a force to be dealt with. The still photographers would select the positions that they thought would be the best places to cover the event. Time after time the big men would barge into the middle of the "stills." Soon, war was declared between the big men and the stills. After time traveling together the two groups got to know each other and the problem was discovered. The producers had told these men that stills knew what was going on and where to be in the best place to get the picture. The producers ordered: Look where the stills go and be there.

Actually, there were two groups of big men on the press charters at that time. The other group had been on the plane for years: the baggage handlers. These men had to be large because you could bring anything on the charters with no regard to size and weight. The networks traveled with hundreds of large "anvil" cases that held lights, extra cameras, chairs, anything. One night these two groups of big men clashed. Loud shouts, a major fight was about to begin, and everyone who had any sense was getting out of harm's way. Hoss, the head of the baggage men, looked into the room of a videoman and saw that he was pumping iron with a full set of barbells. He remembered that the same man had been lifting weights the night before in another country and realized that the weights had been in one of those "anvil' cases" that he had struggled to move from press charter to hotel and back.

All these men earned their money during the coverage of the political conventions. They would lug their rigs around the convention floors and stagger back to their break area. Little network volunteers would cover them with ice to cool them down for a short break and then back to the convention floor.

The biggest man of all was Tiny Ward, the last of the 35mm newsreel cameramen. Even in the sixties there were newsreels in movie theaters in the United States and especially in theaters abroad. He was a giant of a man and a gentleman who was living in an era gone by.

THE POLAROID TEST CAMERA

In addition to the millions of "point and shoot" instant cameras for amateurs, Polaroid made the model 110A. This camera took type 42 black-and-white Polaroid film like the amateur models but had a good-quality compur shutter with shutter speeds and f-stops. It was perfect for photographers using strobe equipment to make a test picture in order to check the quality of their lighting.

Soviet leader Leonid Brezhnev's visit to the United States in 1973 was a major story and *Newsweek* had secured two minutes of his time for a cover portrait session. Photographer Fred Ward and his assistant set the strobes. After several admonitions from Soviet and American handlers that they had just two minutes, Ward was ready. Brezhnev walked into the hotel room and Ward posed his subject, then took his Polaroid test camera and made a quick test picture. He handed the Polaroid to his assistant and started making his *Newsweek* cover portraits.

After a minute, the assistant quietly handed the developed Polaroid print back to Ward so he could make a quick light check. Ward saw that Brezhnev was intrigued by their actions. The test portrait of the Soviet leader looked good and Ward handed Brezhnev the Polaroid print. It was clear that Brezhnev had never seen a Polaroid picture and was amazed by the instant-picture technology. A quick-thinking Ward reached for the Polaroid camera and presented it to the Soviet leader as a gift.

At that point all time limits were off. Brezhnev loved the camera and motioned to his handlers, who were glaring at Ward. A whisper and one was off to another room of the visiting leader's hotel suite. Ward's two minutes turned into five and he created a great selection of photographs for *Newsweek*. The aid hustled back with a little red box and Brezhnev presented it to Ward as his gift of appreciation. The box contained a Soviet-made wrist watch.

Wire services were always looking for a faster delivery system. However, Polaroid film was not the answer.

DIGITAL CAMERAS COME OF AGE

The transition from analog film images to digital images was slow and painful at times. In the eighties scanners replaced enlargers. News photographers developed negative color film and selected the right im-

Ollie Atkins editing his negatives in a makeshift darkroom in French North Africa during World War II. Credit: National Archives.

age to transmit via various proprietary systems like AP's Leafax and transmitted via traditional telephone lines.

In August 1990, President George H.W. Bush sent the 82nd Airborne Division to Saudi Arabia to counter Saddam Hussein's invasion of Kuwait. The Defense Department press pool was activated and instructed to gather at Andrews Air Force Base. Just as he was about to walk out the door of the AP's Washington bureau, Scottie Applewhite was handed a heavy, one-foot-by-two-foot aluminum case. He was told it was a "compander" that made something called a "jpeg image." It came with an inch-thick instruction manual, which Applewhite read in the windowless C-141 on the way to an undisclosed location in Saudi Arabia.

The plane's destination turned out to be Dhahran Air Force Base, which was the center of world attention for the next four months. It took Applewhite a couple of days to get the compander up and running. His first use was the day that the Saudi minders took the pool out to show the strength of the Saudi Air Force. The minder told

Applewhite that he could photograph the American-made F-15's taking off but not the secret hangerbunkers in the background. The photographer promised that the wire photo transmission would be so fuzzy that the bunkers would

Steve Jaffe, Agency France Press, with his exposed roll of film in his mouth reloads his camera during a White House Rose Garden event. Diana Walker in the background. Photo: Dennis Brack.

never be seen. On the front page of the Dhahran newspaper the next morning his photo of the F-15's take-off clearly showed the bunkers. The jpeg compression had resulted in a higher-resolution photograph, a technical advance that did not impress Applewhite's Saudi minders.

DIGITAL CAMERAS WERE COMING

The Mavica

In the eighties the military photographers experimented with a Sony camera named the Mavica. This wonder, the size of a small mailbox, produced images about the quality of the "big foot" images that we see from time to time. Steve Sasson at Kodak built the first CCD-based digital still camera in 1975. Kodak worked with Nikon to develop the DCS 100 SLR, which evolved to a series of what today are low-resolution cameras. These often salmon-colored images improved and the image size increased.

Photographers embraced the new technology. Newspapers loved it. The people at Fuji films and film processing labs did not like it so much.

Digital did deliver pictures to newspapers fast. Ron Edmonds of the Associated

Canon DCS 100

Press used a Nikon Q V-1010T to transmit images of George H.W. Bush taking the presidential oath on January 20, 1989, directly from the camera stand. The competition used film, running it to a trailer on the Capitol grounds, developing the film, scanning, and transmitting. The QV-1010T allowed the AP to beat their competition by thirty minutes.

By the second decade of the twenty-first century, transmitting images directly from the camera had become common. Generally at

Nikon D4

the White House or when the president traveled, the news photographer would make a few frames of the president speaking, put the card with the digital images into a laptop, edit to select the best frame, then send it along with a prepared caption. While the photographer transmitted the images, he or she kept one eye on the president to make sure that a good picture was not missed.

Doug Mills of the *New York Times* sent his images directly to his picture desk via an ftp site. When Mandel Ngan of AFP received the Nikon D4, he learned that each had its own ftp site, allowing him to send his images instantly to AFP editors.

Who knows what is coming tomorrow?

SOURCES

Sources for direct quotes in each chapter are listed below, followed by additional reference material including books, articles, and formal interviews and informal conversations with the author. Publications from the White House News Photographers Association (WHNPA) are listed by subject and year. Many of the events from the Nixon years on were witnessed by the author.

INTRODUCTION: FOOT SOLDIERS OF HISTORY

"Pass Brady": Dorothy Meserve Kunhardt and Philip B. Kunhardt Jr., *Mathew Brady and His World* (Alexandria VA: Time-Life Books, 1997).

"Foot soldiers of history": Hugh Sidey, remarks at opening of WHNPA exhibit at Commerce Department, April 2000.

Also consulted: Mary Panzer, *Mathew Brady and the Image of History* (Washington: Smithsonian, 1997); and Harold Holzer, *Lincoln at Cooper Union: The Speech that Made Abraham Lincoln President* (NY: Simon & Schuster, 2004).

Those 'Picturemen' at the White House

"I try to give you every break": A.E. Scott, "Twenty-five Years and Growing Pains," in WHNPA awards book, 1946.

"You picturemen": WHNPA awards book, 1971.

"The boss is paying you": Woody Wilson, interview with author, April 17, 2007.

"Get it first": Linda Wheeler, "Arthur Ellis, the Picture of Perfection," *Washington Post*, Feb. 12, 1989.

"We went with Harding" and "Why'd you take that picture": Hugh Sidey, "Fifty Years at 1/20 of a Second," in WHNPA Awards Book, 1972

"I do what the photographers ask me": William Seale, ed., *The White House: Actors and Observers* (Boston: Northeastern University Press, 2002).

"Don't worry": Johnny Di Joseph in 1996 as quoted by Jerry Smith in interview with author.

"She came in that grass skirt" and "Wait a minute": Hugh Miller, undated transcript of discussion by Buck May, Hugh Miller, Joe Roberts, and George Dorsey of WHNPA history, conducted by Thomas O'Halloran and Tommy Thompson, WHNPA archives.

"He had a rather square face": Arthur Scott as quoted in book published for the Third Annual Photo Exhibit, WHNPA, 1945.

"Wave, smile, cheer": Edward T. Folliard, "Vive La Golden Compagnie," in WHNPA awards book, 1971.

"He was okay": Johnny Di Joseph to author, Sept. 20, 2000.

"You shall not have one" and "fish will not bite": Hal Elliott, *Hoover, the Fishing President: Portrait of the Private Man and His Life Outdoors* (Mechanicsburg PA: Stackpole Books, 2005).

"Make it snappy": John Faber, *Great News Photos and the Stories Behind Them* (NY: Dover Publications, 1978).

"Up to that time": Transcript, George Tames Oral History Interview, June 11, 1980, Harry S. Truman Presidential Library.

Also consulted: William Hannigan and Ken Johnston, *Picture Machine: The Rise of American Newspictures* (NY: Harry N. Abrams, 2004); Helena Pycior, "The Making of the 'First Dog': President Warren G. Harding and Laddie Boy," *Society and Animals*, Vol. 13, No. 2 (2005); Transcript, General Frederic B. Butler Oral History Interview, Oct. 6, 1967, Herbert Hoover Presidential Library; Howell Raines, *Fly Fishing Through the Midlife Crisis* (NY: William Morrow, 1993); and minutes of WHNPA meetings, Jan. 12, 1929, and March 11, 1932.

THE GREATEST PICTURE SUBJECT OF ALL

"President Roosevelt is crippled"; "You follow the rules"; "So the photographers agreed"; "Let's try one": George Tames Oral History Interview, HSTL.

"No movies of me" and "If, as it happened": Hugh Gregory Gallagher, *FDR's Splendid Deception* (NY: Dodd, Meade, 1985).

"I asked once": George Tames, *Eye On Washington: The Presidents Who've Known Me* (NY: HarperCollins, 1990).

"Daring and fearlessness": A.J. Ezickson, *Get That Picture! The Story of the News Cameraman* (NY: National Library Press, 1938).

"It's pictures we're after" and "It was seldom": WHNPA awards book, May 1945.

"Thank you, Mr. President": Max Desfor to author, informal conversation. Desfor was among photographers who remembered Thompson's trick.

"Max, get your ass back here": Max Desfor, interview with author, Feb. 26, 2012.

"I've seen things": Edward Widdis, WHNPA newsletter, The Press, April 1943. Material about McNamara and Forsythe also came from this newsletter issue.

Bert Brandt material: *Washington News*, June 7, 1944.

"Where's Sammy?": "Press Flashes," *Popular Photography*, May 1943.

"How about a picture?": *Washington Times Herald*, July 16 and 17, 1944.

Also consulted: Henry D. Burroughs, *Close-Ups of History: Three Decades Through the Lens of an AP Photographer* (Columbia: University of Missouri Press, 2007); Woodrow "Woody" Wilson, interview with author, April 7, 2007; Thomas Fleming, *The New Dealers' War: FDR and the War Within World War II* (NY: Basic Books, 2001); Maxine T. Edwards, "Portrait of a Photojournalist," in *Jackie Martin: The Washington Years*, exhibition catalog edited by Amy S. Doherty (Syracuse NY: Syracuse University, 1986); Margaret Frances Thomas, "Through the Lens of Experience: American Women Newspaper Photographers" (Master's thesis, University of Texas, 2007); and Robert Klara, *FDR's Funeral Train: A Betrayed Widow, a Soviet Spy, and a Presidency in the Balance* (NY: Palgrave Macmillan, 2010).

OUT OF THE DOG HOUSE

"I forgot something": Max Desfor, interview with author, Jan. 7, 2008.

"Where are the photographers" and "You know, George": Tames oral history, HSTPL.

"Photographers have to make" and "It's good exercise": "Remembering Marion Carpenter," Associated Press, Nov. 25, 2002.

"He was the sort": Wilson interview with author.

"Covering Truman": Jim Atherton, interview with author, Oct. 22, 2009.

"These are the best friends": Arnold Sachs, interview with author, May 5, 2000.

"Here's an exclusive": "Lady of the Press: She Spilled Bean Soup on Writer on Purpose," *Washington Post*, March 25, 1949.

Blair House events: Maurice Johnson to author, informal conversation.

"Hello, Mr. President": Burroughs, *Close-Ups of History*.

"Just look over": Gerald Clarke, Janice Simpson, Elizabeth Rudolph, "Images: Freezing Moments in History," *Time*, Dec. 28, 1981.

"Al, take it easy": Tames Oral History, HSTPL.

"And I still remember": George Tames to author, who witnessed the event that day, in informal conversation.

"Listen, you know": Floyd M. Boring Oral History Interview, Sept. 21, 1988, HSTPL.

"Al, I hear": Vince Finnigan in interview with author, Oct. 23, 2002.

"George, there were so many": George Skadding, unpublished and undated notes, in WHNPA archives.

"Covering Mr. Truman": Folliard, "Vive La Golden Compagnie."

"I hearby declare": Sachs interview with author.

Also consulted: WHNPA Newsletter, Vol. IV, No. 1, February 1946; and Jonathan Daniels, *White House Witness, 1942-1945* (Garden City NY: Doubleday, 1975).

GIVING THEM THE PICTURES THEY WANT

"Now I know" and "The general says": Henry Griffin, WHNPA awards book, 1970.

"The easel fell": Helen Thomas, "Photographers I have Known," WHNPA awards book, 1974.

"I did not assume": Text of Eisenhower's speech to Senate and House, *New York Times*, Feb. 2, 1951.

"Too damn much trouble": General Craig Cannon Oral History Interview, April 5, 1975, Dwight D. Eisenhower Presidential Library.

"Ike had a funny thing": Burroughs, *Close-Ups of History.*

"Ike hired the best": Jim Atherton, interview with author, Oct. 22, 2009.

"You always knew": Arnold Sachs interview with author.

"Listen, Mr. Haggerty": James Haggerty, "I Like the White House Photogs," in WHNPA awards book, 1955.

"Be sure to be here": Arnold Sachs interview with author.

"The president wants to talk": Dave Wiegman to author, informal conversation.

"Ike would make": Arnold Sachs interview with author.

"Where's Jr.?": Tom Cravens Jr., interview with author, Sept. 14, 2002.

"What are you doing here?": John Cochran to author, informal conversation.

Also consulted: Peter Carlson, *K Blows His Top: A Cold War Comic Interlude Starring Nikita Khrushchev, America's Most Unlikely Tourist* (NY: PublicAffairs, 2009).

Why They Made That Picture

"They're not going": *The Memories: JFK, 1961-1963, of Cecil Stoughton, the President's Photographer, and Major General Chester V. Clifton, the President's Military Aide* (NY: Norton, 1973).

"We had arranged": Gary Haynes, email to author, Sept. 5, 2011.

"Why did you publish": Tames, *Eye on Washington.*

"I wonder where": Tames oral interview, HSTPL.

Sock drawer: George Tames to author, informal conversation.

Heiberger and Mrs. Kennedy: Heiberger to author, informal conversation.

"Why did you": Arnold Sachs interview with author.

"I thought that" and "Things get kind of sticky": Michael O'Brien: *John F. Kennedy: A Biography* (NY: Thomas Dunne, 2005).

"Must be a Texas salute" and "Then we heard": Burroughs, *Close-Ups of History.*

"Why don't you give": Gerald Blaine and Lisa McCubbin, *The Kennedy Detail: JFK's Secret Service Agents Break Their Silence* (NY: Gallery Books, 2010).

"What are you talking about" and other material on salute photo: Stan Stearns, interview with author, March 9, 2011.

Also consulted: Gretchen Craft Rubin, *Forty Ways to Look at JFK* (NY: Ballantine, 2005); William Manchester, *The Death of a President, November 20-November 25, 1963* (NY: Harper & Row, 1967); Cecil Stoughton Oral History Interview, March 1, 1971, Lyndon B. Johnson Presidential Library; George Tames Oral History Interview, Jan. 13, 1988, United States Senate Historical Office; Joe O'Donnell obituary, *New York Times*, Aug. 15, 2007, and subsequent corrections published Sept. 5 and 15, 2007.

That Was Just LBJ

"Because of military secrecy" and "Arranging things": Robert A. Caro, *Means of Ascent* (NY: Knopf, 1990).

"So the male photographers": Margaret Frances Thomas, "Through the Lens of Experience: American Women Newspaper Photographers" (Master's thesis, University of Texas, 2007).

"Charlie, why did you:" Charlie Gory to author, shortly after incident.

"Jim, did you make": Jim Atherton, interview with author, May 2007.

"Bryon, you got": Bryon Schumaker, interview with author, August 2010.

"If you ever" and "Shoot that thing": Frank Johnston to author, informal conversation.

"I want you": George Tames to author, informal conversation.

"Roddey, the president wants you": a story told around the White House for decades.

"If you're going to Texas": John Dreylinger, interview with author, April 23, 2010.

"He was calm": Hugh Sidey, "The Presidency," *Time*, Aug. 2, 1982.

"You know, if this plane": a story told around the White House for years.

"Get me that Jap": Tames, *Eye on Washington.*

"Oke had class": Howard Chapnick, *Truth Needs No Ally: Inside Photojournalism* (Columbia: University of Missouri Press, 1984).

"You can't keep": Johnson, in presence of author.

Also consulted: Joe Laitin obituary, *New York Times*, Jan. 21, 2002; Leigh Kelley, "Resident's Photographs Tell Presidential Stories," *Hendersonville (N.C.) News*, Feb. 21, 2005.

Do You Like Your Job?

"They should have told me": James Wooten, "Visible Photographer Loses U.S. Job: In Nixon Background," *New York Times*, Feb. 28, 1973.

"Let us set aside": James Deakin, *Straight Stuff: The Reporters, the White House, and the Truth* (NY: Morrow, 1984).

"Everyone played" and "Well, I'll have a drink": Henry Burroughs, "Downstairs at 1600," in WHNPA award book, 1971.

"For a Washington reporter": Hugh Sidey to author, informal conversation.

"Do you like your job?": Douglas Hallett, "A Low-level Memoir of the Nixon White House," *New York Times Magazine*, Oct. 20, 1974.

"Young man": John Full to author, informal conversation.

"Now would be a good time": George Christian to author, November 2011.

Not a Typical President

"He had a style": Fred Ward, interviewed on "The Early Show" on CBS, Feb. 11, 2009.

"Have you been keeping": Ford, in presence of author.

"I think Cleve": Fred Ward to author, informal conversation.

"The press was determined": *Newsweek*, Oct. 18, 1976.

Also consulted: John W. "Bill" Roberts, audio diary, July-September 1974, Gerald R. Ford Presidential Library.

Very Frustrating Times

"The first line of defense": Jody Powell, Oral History Interview, Dec. 17, 1981, Miller Center Foundation, University of Virginia.

"Sorry, I'm on deadline": Angie Cannon, "A Pretend Reporter Covered the White House to Age 84," *Seattle Times*, May 7, 1985.

Also consulted: Ronald Kessler, *In the President's Secret Service: Behind the Scenes with Agents in the Line of Fire and the Presidents They Protect* (NY: Random House, 2009).

A Couple of Regular Guys

"How about clipping": Edmonds to author, informal conversation.

"Due to the crowds": radio transmission overheard by author.

"When the first shot": Ron Edmonds, Associated Press video interview, March 30, 2011.

"Thank you, Chief": source who wishes to remain anonymous, in informal conversation with author.

Also consulted: Joseph Petro with Jeffrey Robinson, *Standing Next to History: An Agent's Life Inside the Secret Service* (NY: Thomas Dunne, 2005); Larry Downing, "George H.W. Bush: Old School President Top in 'Class,'" on Photographers Blog, Reuters website, July 7, 2011.

THE NEXT GENERATION

"I was standing" and other Walker anecdotes: Diana Walker, email to author, March 2013.

"Ladies and gentlemen": Ken Blaylock, interview with author, Jan. 7, 2012.

"If looks could kill": Bob Bramson to author, May 2011.

HEROES

George looked like your uncle: Wilson interview with author.

"Mr. Harris, I'm amazed": John Farber, "A Recorder of Presidential History," in WHNPA awards book, 1958.

"Motor drives": Jim Atherton interview with author, Nov. 12, 2010.

"All you have to do": Toby Massey, "Washington Recap," in WHNPA awards book, 1970.

"Mr. Secretary" and "Al, take it easy": Tames Oral History, HSTPL.

"Life magazine put together": Gene Roberts and Hank Klibanoff, *The Race Beat: The Press, the Civil Rights Struggle, and the Awakening of a Nation* (NY: Knopf, 2006);

Life staff party: Hugh Sidey to author, Dec. 12, 2002.

"You have to have shadows" and "They're all posed": Jim Atherton, interview with author, Dec. 6, 2011.

"Just like the way": Dennis Brack and David Burnett, "Athertonisms," *The Report*, WHNPA, March 2012.

"What about our families?" and other Wiegman anecdotes: Wiegman to author, informal conversation.

"Did we get it?": Fielman interview with WUSA, March 30, 2011.

"What's new?" and other Halstead anecdotes: Halstead to author, informal conversation.

"One thing I remember" and other Walker anecdotes: Walker email to author.

"*Newsweek* New York wired me" and other McNamee anecdotes: McNamee to author, informal conversation.

Also consulted: Gerald Clarke, Janice Simpson, Elizabeth Rudolph, "Images: Freezing Moments in History," *Time*, Dec. 28, 1981; "New Angle on Lincoln," *U.S. Camera*, May 1960; Edwards, "Portrait of a Photojournalist"; Thomas, "Through the Lens of Experience"; Alice Rogers Hager, "Jackie Martin Escapes Unhurt as Plane Crashes in Brazil," *Washington Times Herald*, Aug. 20, 1941; and "Jackie Martin Hired by War Department to Snap WAAC's in Ft. Des Moines," *Washington Times Herald*, July 16, 1942; and Dirck Halstead, *Moments in Time: Photos and Stories from One of America's Top Photojournalists* (NY: Abrams, 2006).

CONCLUSION: SOMETIMES LIFE IS SWEET

Tames drops his lens: George Tames to author, informal conversation.

Tom Craven Sr. and the Hindenburg: Tom Craven Jr. to author, informal conversation.

Charlie Corte: Arnold Sach interview with author and WHNPA meeting notes, June 1962, WHNPA archives.

Lighting the RFK funeral: Bernie Roberts to author, informal conversation.

"Tell you what"; "Get the underlings"; and "Close the door": heard by author during event.

"Sir, you dropped something": Downing to author, informal conversation.

"I hesitated": Walker email to author.

A Look at Photographers' Tools

Wet plate process: Rob Gibson, a wet plate collodoin photographer, explained and demonstrated the process to author.

"We were always in a tizzy": "Ike Retires," WHNPA newsletter, February 1954.

"A little more zip": Jack Shields to author, informal conversation.

"You'd be surprised": Wilson, interview with author.

Weegee anecdote: Herb Schwartz, interview with author, May 2011.

"Funny thing": a story long told by photographers.

"Is that a new one?": A.E. Scott, "Twenty-five Years and Growing Pains," in WHNPA awards book, 1946.

"You can click" and "When the news press types": Tames Oral History, HSTPL.

"My light is right here": John Mazziotta to author, informal conversation.

"Cleve, how long": Atherton interview with author, Nov. 15, 2011

Also consulted: Joyce Wadler, "Born 150 Years Too Late, *New York Times*, Aug. 3, 2006; Naomi Rosenblum, *A World History of Photography*, 3rd ed. (NY: Abbeville, 1997); Roy Meredith, *Mr. Lincoln's Camera Man: Mathew B. Brady*, 2nd rev. ed. (NY: Dover, 1974); Harvey S. Teal, *Partners With the Sun: South Carolina Photographers, 1840-1940* (Columbia SC: University of South Carolina, 2000); Frederic Eugene Ives, *Autobiography of an Amateur Inventor* (Philadelphia: Private printing, 1928); Hugh Miller, "Photographic Memories," WHNPA Seventh Annual Awards Book; Chapnick, *Truth Needs No Ally*; William E. Inman Sr., "Grafacts," in *Graflex Historic Quarterly*, Vol. 13, Issue 1 (Winter 2008); and C. Zoe Smith, "Black Star Picture Agency: Life's European Connection," *Journalism History*, Vol. 13, No. 1 (Spring 1986).

Index